THE ART OF MAKING MAGAZINES

Columbia Journalism Review Books

Series Editors: Victor Navasky, Evan Cornog, Mike Hoyt, and the editors of the *Columbia Journalism Review*

Columbia Journalism Review Books

Series Editors: Victor Navasky, Evan Cornog, Mike Hoyt, and the editors of the *Columbia Journalism Review*

For more than fifty years, the *Columbia Journalism Review* has been the gold standard for media criticism, holding the profession to the highest standards and exploring where journalism is headed, for good and for ill.

Columbia Journalism Review Books expands upon this mission, seeking to publish titles that allow for greater depth in exploring key issues confronting journalism, both past and present, and pointing to new ways of thinking about the field's impact and potential.

Drawing on the expertise of the editorial staff at the *Columbia Journalism Review* as well as the Columbia Journalism School, the series of books will seek out innovative voices as well as reclaim important works, traditions, and standards. In doing this, the series will also incorporate new ways of publishing made available by the Web and e-books.

edited by Victor S. Navasky and Evan Cornog

THE ART OF MAKING MAGAZINES

On Being an Editor and Other Views from the Industry

Columbia University Press New York

Columbia University Press
Publishers Since 1893
New York   Chichester, West Sussex
cup.columbia.edu

Library of Congress Cataloging-in-Publication Data
The art of making magazines : on being an editor and other views from the industry /
    edited by Victor S. Navasky and Evan Cornog.
    p.   cm. — (Columbia journalism review books)
ISBN 978-0-231-13136-0 (cloth : alk. paper) — ISBN 978-0-231-13137-7 (pbk.) —
    ISBN 978-0-231-50469-0 (electronic)
1. Journalism—Editing. 2. Periodicals—Publishing. I. Navasky, Victor S. II. Cornog, Evan.
PN4778.A78 2012
070.4′1—dc23   2011044351

Columbia University Press books are printed on permanent and durable acid-free paper.
This book was printed on paper with recycled content.
Printed in the United States of America

c 10 9 8 7 6 5 4
p 10 9 8 7 6 5 4 3 2 1

Contents

Introduction

John Gregory Dunne began his Delacorte lecture on February 14, 2003, by observing that "in general, it is bad business for writers to talk about writing. William Faulkner once said that a writer's obituary should read, 'he wrote the books, and then he died.'"

Dunne died before the year was out, but as you will see from his talk, at least as far as his meditation on the writer's voice was concerned, he was wrong. No point in summarizing what he had to say here, because a) his nuanced, careful prose does not easily lend itself to paraphrase; and b) you can turn to page 1 and read it for yourself. Nevertheless, as a preview of coming attractions, we can conceive of no better prelude to this collection of ruminations on magazine journalism than Dunne's observation that "the fact of the matter is that as you get older, you will discover that the singer is more important than the song. If you do magazine journalism, 'why' ultimately matters as much as or even more than 'who,' 'what,' 'where,' 'when,' and 'how.' And not so much 'why' as a meditation on 'why.' Or a contemplation on 'how' and 'who.'"

The lectures that follow are part of a series originally aimed at students at Columbia University's Graduate School of Journalism who have chosen to concentrate on magazines. Their purpose: to provide insight into the world of magazines by way of the perspectives of those who write, publish, edit, and design them.

This is not a how-to book, but it is, in many respects, a how-to-think-about-it book. At the loftiest level, one might think of magazines as what Francis Bacon, the philosopher, who helped clarify the difference between analytic (deductive) and inductive reasoning, meant when he referred to "the middle axiom." As Bacon saw it, analytic reasoning starts at the highest level of abstraction, whereas inductive reasoning proceeds from the bottom up. Notwithstanding journals of opinion (like *The Nation* and *National Review*) or magazines of ideas (like *Harper's* and *The Atlantic*), magazines as a genre do not specialize in abstract generalities; nor, at the other extreme, do they merely present raw, undigested experience. Rather, their comparative advantage is in dealing with the in-between or netherworld—the middle region, inhabited, according to Bacon, by "the solid and living axioms on which depend the affairs and the fortunes of men."

As the talks below demonstrate, magazines as a class, be they magazines of ideas, journals of opinion, newsweeklies, or niche publications about matters culinary, athletic, sexual, or what have you, by definition reflect the values and tensions of the culture and society they help to define. And the crazy quilt of perspectives and backgrounds represented by those whose thoughts appear below help explain why magazines and the people who run them are still, and perhaps always will be, in the middle of their journey.

For example, Bob Gottlieb, who had served as editor-in-chief of Alfred A. Knopf, one of America's most distinguished book publishing enterprises, before he became the first post–William Shawn editor of *The New Yorker*, one of America's most distinguished magazines, provides a unique perspective on the job of magazine editor by looking at it through a book publisher's lens:

> You are there to keep the writer happy and feeling that he or she is
> protected ... which means they have to believe that their editor ...
> understands their work, sympathizes with their work, and is on

their wavelength. They must believe that the editor can make the book not other than what it is, but better than what it is. . . . When you're the editor-in-chief of a magazine . . . it's opposite. You are the living god. You are not there to please the writers, but the writers are there to satisfy you because they want to be in the magazine, and you are the one who says yes or no.

The lectures contain foxy perceptions like Ruth Reichl's casual observation that tables of contents are moving back farther and farther and farther in magazines because advertisers pay more to be in front of the table of contents. They also contain hedgehoggy ones, like Tina Brown quoting Elizabeth Hardwick on how "magazines are like mushrooms. They should grow in the dark." Translation: the reader, who is comfortable with things the way they have always been, should not be traumatized by change. (So the trick is to change things without appearing to change them.)

In the spring of 1971, on the occasion of his departure as editor-in-chief of *Harper's Magazine,* Willie Morris famously referred to the struggle between the money men and the literary men ("As always," he lamented, "the money men won"). And Rick MacArthur, in his account of his own life as the publisher of *Harper's* some years later, seems to incarnate the dilemma, although as the ostensible money man his heart is clearly on the literary side. But of course there are other, no less important divides at the core of magazine making.

Vide, the tension between the word people and the art people. As Chris Dixon, design director of *Vanity Fair,* observes, "A lot of times . . . [the art people] will put together a presentation of how we're going to visualize [a story], and the editor will say, 'Well, if you had read it, you would have known da, da, da.' So they're assuming [wrongly] that we haven't read the piece and we don't understand."

And then there is the fashion magazine editor who reports that most editors learned that "pictures are things that happened down there with the cool people in the art department, and photos were merely visual support for the words."

I learned the differences between the two kinds of people who go into magazine editorial, the words people and the visual people, and woe be to the editor who doesn't understand the primal attachment those in both camps have to the superiority of their point of view. It's usually the words people who end up being editor-in-chief, which is interesting because at the big national glossies, most of the budget is spent on photography.

This raises the still open question of how the primacy of the image will fare in the age of the Internet. Roberta Myers, who worked for *Rolling Stone*, *Interview*, and *Seventeen*, among other magazines, before she arrived at *Elle*, where she is editor-in-chief, recalls, "Somebody told me that if I needed resources and money for *Elle*, all I had to do was go to the 45th floor (where the CEO sits) and yell 'digital,' and they'd throw a pile of money at me."

Although several of the talks represented here were delivered in the pre-Internet era, they seem inevitably to anticipate the key issues that confront magazines in the online world. One of the editors of this volume recently undertook a survey of "magazines and their Web sites" and discovered—surprise, surprise—that given online's presumed need for speed (in order to gain the traffic coveted by advertisers), many magazine Web sites are not fact-checked or copyedited with the rigor of their parent magazine, if at all, and the church-state separation between editorial content and advertising is, for the most part, honored in the breach.

Peter Canby, who oversees *The New Yorker*'s much-vaunted fact-checking process, recalls that when he was first hired as a checker, the managing editor told him that fact-checking was the best way to learn the basics of journalism. What then does this say about those magazine sites that do no fact-checking at all?

And Canby makes the interesting case that rigorous fact-checking does more than prevent errors from appearing in the magazine. As he puts it, "the checking department attempts to ask really critical questions, to look at logic, at the flaws in arguments, and to try to get these things addressed so that what ultimately appears in the magazine does have this texture of freshness and originality and accuracy. This not only gives the magazine its credibility but also imparts a distinctive quality to *The New Yorker* prose."

In other words, as *The Atlantic*'s longtime copy chief, Barbara Walraff, says apropos of copyediting, "a magazine needs someone, or a team of people, who work on everything and make sure it meets all their standards." And since there are no universal English-language standards, or even consistent American English standards, "each magazine has to make choices . . . each choice says a little bit of something about the identity of the magazine."

Too bad we all can't have the benefit of Walrath's explanations why *The Atlantic* chose this rather than that in each instance. But she does share the advice *Atlantic* editor Bill Whitworth gave on hiring her as copy chief: that she should always write little explanations on the galleys of the reasons for changes, and that she should always suggest a fix, "not just circle something and write 'awkward' with a question mark next to it."

Are online magazines really magazines? That, of course, is a question that hovers over any comparison of old and "new" (now called "digital") media. The answer may be found between the lines of the contributions of both Tina Brown and Ruth Reichl, each of whom gave two lectures— one before, and one after the advent of the Internet. They each describe before and after from very different vantage points.

There is one point on which most of the contributors to these ruminations on Bacon's middle axiom seem to agree: that ultimately a magazine's identity is determined by its readers. This may sound like a truism, but the various paths taken to arrive at that conclusion suggest it is anything but. Thus, Felix Dennis, the one-time proprietor of *Maxim* and current boss of *The Week*, is eloquent in his sermon on why "the reader is king."

And the late Michael Kelly, who went on to edit *The New Republic* and *The Atlantic*, tells of starting out as a writer when *Playboy* commissioned him to travel the country writing about sex, at a time when sex seemed to be coming out all over. A talented writer, he wandered the sex circuit interviewing the male beneficiaries of the new openness, and found what seemed to him "a rather grim place filled with grim, sad men, pathetic really, engaged in a kind of dismal and pathetic pursuit." When he finally turned in his essay, his editor told him, "You really captured something here, and you've really got down on paper the sheer awfulness of these guys' lives, how sad and lonely and pathetic they are." Kelly said, "Thank you very much." His editor then added, "At *Playboy* we have a term for these men." And Kelly said, "Really?" And he said, "Yes, we call them our readers."

Evan Cornog
Victor Navasky

THE ART OF MAKING MAGAZINES

1

Talking About Writing for Magazines (Which One Shouldn't Do)

John Gregory Dunne was a novelist, essayist, screenwriter (with his wife, Joan Didion), and critic. His books include *True Confessions, Dutch Shea, Jr.*, and *Playland*, and he was a regular contributor to the *New York Review of Books*. He died in December 2003.

In general, it is bad business for a writer to talk about writing. William Faulkner once said that a writer's obituary should read, "He wrote the books, then he died."

Allowing for the Faulkner caveat, let me state a few basic precepts. I am a writer. I am a professional writer. I write to make a living. That is what I do. I do it the same way some people make their living as lawyers or teachers or executives or engineers or investment analysts or doctors or contractors or entrepreneurs or bureaucrats, or even as remittance men. Writing is my job. It is the only job I have. I don't teach on the side, I rarely lecture—and when I do, it's usually free, like this one.

I have been asked this evening if I would talk about a writer's voice. All of you here tonight are enterprising young journalists and you believe in facts and who, what, where, when, and how, and everything will open up and lay itself out.

If it's not Enron.

The fact of the matter is that as you get older, you will discover that the singer is more important than the song. If you do magazine journalism, "why" ultimately matters as much as or even more than "who," "what," "where," "when," and "how." And not so much "why" as a meditation on "why." Or a contemplation on "how" or "who."

When I say the singer is more important than the song, I don't mean in the sense of ego. I mean you bring more to the story. You bring an attitude. You bring a professional and personal DNA. You are smarter. You know more. You have more filed away in your memory drum that you think you have forgotten. You have the odd fact stashed away, you didn't even know it was there, it's the fact that demolishes received wisdom.

An example:

A couple of years ago, in 1999 or 2000, I wrote a piece for *The New Yorker* called "Virtual Patriotism." It was about the surfeit of patriotism that supposedly took over the land when *Saving Private Ryan* was released, as if you can find patriotism at the Cineplex, in your five-dollar bucket of butter-flavored popcorn and three-dollar box of Milk Duds.

There was all this "greatest generation" bullshit: those guys were tough, we're soft, we're the Seinfeld generation. I thought the op-ed page posturing had the air of generational flagellation lite. There was also a lot of specious nonsense about the Vietnam generation: those guys wouldn't fight for their country, we would be proud to.

It's not unlike what we hear today, the confusion of patriotism with cheerleading. But that's another subject.

Anyway, I remembered something, and this is what I wrote:

The strength of this delusion is such that it survived even the Gulf War. In February 1991, David Maraniss of *The Washington Post* interviewed seven male Vanderbilt University undergraduates about Operation Desert Storm. All were twenty or twenty-one years old, roughly the same age as the troops poised to liberate Kuwait and invade Iraq. Five of the seven supported the war, none was willing to fight in it, and all were opposed to military conscription. "This might sound selfish, but I think it would be a shame to put America's best young minds on the front line," said one, and another, "I don't see myself shooting a gun . . . I don't feel I could be an effective soldier."

On the op-ed page of the *Los Angeles Times*, a Princeton senior was even more unequivocal in his espousal of student entitlement, and his acceptance of the idea that America now had a Hessian class that would fight this and future wars, an army of the socially and economically disenfranchised drawn from the skid rows of the American dream. "Is it hypocritical of me to support the Persian Gulf War in which some of my peers are dying, but not be willing to put my life on the line?" he wrote. "I don't think so. . . . No one is arguing that our volunteer troops are expendable. But we should be willing to risk their lives even when our immediate security is not on the line. After all, they agreed to be used that way."

"What the Gulf War"—and this is still from my *New Yorker* piece— "showed was that 'support,' or enthusiasm, for war now rises in inverse proportion to the inclination to fight it."

Here is the point I am trying to make. I wrote this piece, as I said, in 1999; David Maraniss did his piece in *The Washington Post* in 1991. Eight years earlier. But I remembered it. I also remembered that Princeton asshole (in part because I went to Princeton). That's what I mean when I say you are smarter. When I stashed this stuff either in my mind or on a computer or in a file box, I had no idea I was one day going to find a place for it. But it was there and allowed me to question this dreamy idea of patriotism.

One more example, from a piece my wife wrote for *The New York Review of Books* about the Central Park jogger.

You all remember the jogger story. It was 1989, and this young woman, a thirty-year-old broker in a big downtown firm, was jogging in the park after dark, and she was attacked, raped, and nearly killed—brained with a brick, her brain tissue exposed by a group of young blacks from Harlem who brought the word "wilding" into the language.

It was a ghastly story. But what interested Joan was the way that all stories in New York had to have a sentimental narrative, that the city was a cesspool of sentimentality, that even the tragic and the horrific, as this story was, had to be turned into a morality tale, a parable: courage and class, indomitable dignity.

Here is a paragraph from that piece:

> The narrative comforts us, in other words, with the assurance that the world is knowable, even flat, and New York its center, its motor, its dangerous but vital "energy." "Family in Fatal Mugging Loved New York" was the *Times* headline on a story following the September murder, in the 53rd Street IND station, of a twenty-two-year-old tourist from Utah. The young man, his parents, his brother and his sister-in-law had attended the U.S. Open and were reportedly on their way to dinner at Tavern on the Green. "New York, to them, was the greatest place in the world," a family friend from Utah was quoted as having said. Since the narrative requires that the rest of the country provide a dramatic contrast to New York, the family's hometown in Utah was characterized by the *Times* as a place where "life revolves around the orderly rhythms of Brigham Young University" and "there is only about one murder a year." The town was in fact Provo, a mean frontier town where the Central Pacific met the Union Pacific and Gary Gilmore shot the motel manager, both in life and in Norman Mailer's *The Executioner's Song*.

She remembered Provo, was able to retrieve it from her memory drum in order to expose the sentimentality behind the "Family in Fatal Mugging" headline and the equally sentimental celebration of Provo's neighborly values perfection in the *Times* story, because twelve years earlier she had read *The Executioner's Song* and reviewed it for the *New York Times Book Review*.

These two examples are what I mean when I say that with age and experience you bring a professional DNA to a story.

Let's get to the personal DNA.

I'd like to quote here from the English novelist, the late Paul Scott. He wrote *The Raj Quartet*, in my mind the best book—a tetrology, actually—

to come out of World War II. This is what he wrote in a book called *On Writing*:

> I am someone born in my age, subject to its pressures, prejudices and expectations, scorched by its past, living in its present.

I don't think anyone has ever explained better what makes a writer. Not just a writer of fiction, but any writer. And explained where the writer's voice comes from. Let me repeat it: "Born in my age, subject to its pressures, prejudices and expectations, scorched by its past." "The duty of the writer"—this is Paul Scott again—"is to expose to public view his private view of what reality is." Because everything the writer writes is only an extended metaphor of his view of life.

You bring to this extended metaphor a childlike curiosity. For example, I am interested in how things work, in how a deal is made, a conglomerate formed. How a tooth is reconstructed or an aorta patched. How Mariano Rivera throws a hard slider, how the air currents and the speed of the projectile and the angle of the wrist at the point of release conspire to make a pitch that one man was not intended to throw, and that another man cannot hit.

I guess that what I am trying to say is that being a writer is a license to be curious.

Beyond that, "the hours are good," as Ernest Hemingway once said. And as John McNulty added, "There's no heavy lifting."

A personal note here, my own DNA, as it were. I don't think I would have become a writer if I hadn't stuttered (or stammered) as a child. A stutterer is by definition an outsider. A stutterer is not a CEO. Or an adviser on decedent trusts or fiduciary management. A stutterer cannot be a brain surgeon if it takes him eight or ten seconds to ask for a clamp.

I still stutter, although I can usually disguise it so well that—unless I am drunk or tired or nervous—the stammer is almost imperceptible.

Like all stutterers, I have my own distant early warning system. I can recognize two or three sentences ahead those hard consonants that will trigger the booby traps, and I have a warehouse of soft and sibilant synonyms that will carry me across the minefields of speech.

As you have noticed, the effect of this personal early warning line is to give my diction an odd, herky-jerky cadence, making me sound like nothing so much as a simultaneous translation from another language into English.

And so, because of this stammer, I considered myself one of those who ends up as an outcast, an adventurer, a malcontent, a ne'er-do-well.

In compensation, I learned to express myself on paper. I listened to the way people talked, becoming in the process a rather good mimic, and grew so precociously observant that my dear late mother once complained that I never missed a twitch or a wonky eyelid or a crooked seam on a stocking.

When I was a young writer, I thought this facility a virtue, but as I grow older I am less sure. Put a writer with a tendency toward misanthropy in front of a typewriter and the possibility—the probability—exists that someone, usually someone unsuspecting, is going to get mugged.

I recognize an occasional absence of charity in myself—the writer as malcontent, remember—and for this reason I started to put myself into my work. Perhaps if I exposed my own mosaic of petty treasons, the people I was writing about would have less reason to complain.

You see, no matter what the writer is writing about, no matter where his curiosity takes him, the writer is always essentially investigating himself. He is always trying to reprogram the responses to his own past.

I can tell you who this writer is. I was a stammerer, which already in my own mind made me an outcast. I was also Irish and a Catholic, and in a real sense, in the New England city where I grew up, that made me a social outcast. This was in the years before Jack Kennedy was elected president. It will be difficult for many of you to believe now how his election in 1960 was a kind of absolution, in certain parts of New England, for having been born Irish and Catholic.

We did not know Protestants. We did not know Jews. Not to mention blacks. When my wife and I were married, my mother had a reception for us in Hartford, my hometown. There were 125 people there. One hundred and twenty-four were Irish Catholics. The 125th was my wife, who was Episcopalian—and worse, a Californian.

My grandfather was an immigrant from County Roscommon, twelve years old when he washed up in Hartford in 1869, with a card around his neck to identify him to relatives from an earlier generation of refugees. His education ended in the fifth grade. From 1874 until his death in 1940, he was a grocer in Frog Hollow, a section of Hartford that the poor Irish who lived there would be too proud to call a ghetto, its proper description.

Frog Hollow abutted Park Street, and was a community of male Irish laborers and female Irish domestics who worked farther west in the households of people I still call, with a special distaste not allayed by my years, Yanks; "WASP" belongs to the sanitized diction of pop anthropology. For the Irish in Frog Hollow, upward mobility was available only via what I once called "the three Ps—politics, the priesthood, and the police department."

I grew up in West Hartford, the ne plus ultra of the Hartford Irish immigrant dream, steerage to suburbia in three generations. My grandfather had prospered, and my parents' house on Albany Avenue had a six-car garage. Ours was a world of Havilland china and private schools and a retinue of help—I am still not assimilated enough to use the word "servants."

I became a cloned Yank. My father graduated from Catholic University and Harvard Medical School—guess where he said he was educated—and I had a Princeton degree and a jaded sophistication much valued at Hartford debutante parties.

A Hartford debutante—that seems to me the definition of an oxymoron.

I not only wanted to be assimilated, I was ashamed of being Irish.

Blessedly, the cultural transplant did not take place. The gutter Irish spleen rejected the faux Yank cells. I was, I remain, ineffably Frog Hollow. Today I remember the nuns who taught me at St. Joseph School—Sister Barnabas, Sister Theodosius, Sister Marie de Nice—more clearly than I remember the professors in the history department at Princeton.

The Sisters of Mercy who ran St. Joseph were like steelworkers. If they had been born men, they would have had tattoos of the Sacred

Heart on their biceps and worn T-shirts with a deck of smokes rolled up in the sleeve. Sister Robert was the ringleader. She had a red face and rimless glasses and an 18-inch ruler that she swung as if she were a Crusader, and the kids in her homeroom were a bunch of infidels.

The line on Sister Robert was that she would hit you until you bled, and then she would hit you for bleeding. If that didn't work, there was always Father Hannon, the principal, who was a mean man with a rubber hose. This led to a rather sullen bunch of malcontents in the school yard, where your status was based on the number of times Father Hannon bent you over the refectory table in his office, made you lower your knickers, and whacked you on your bare ass with his rubber hose. We had not heard of the word "pedophilia" in those days.

The true Irish voice of my generation is the voice of a man with a chip on his shoulder the size of a California redwood. Let me emphasize that a voice does not have to be nice, and if the voice belongs to someone of Irish extraction, it rarely is. I think this comes from an inbred hatred of the Brits, and by extension a distaste for all Protestants.

The Irish voice is essentially one that gets a boot out of frailty and misfortune; its comedy is the comedy of the small mind and the mean spirit. Nothing lifts the heart of the Irish caroler more than the small vice, the tiny lapse, the exposed vanity, the recherché taste.

Although it is not necessary for the writer to be a prick, neither does it hurt. The writer is an eternal outsider, his nose pressed against whatever window on the other side of which he sees his material. Resentment sharpens his eye, hostility hones his killer instinct. And I guess what I am also trying to say is that while a writer's past is always there, it has to be mined, dug out, held up against the light. It does not extrude naturally from the subconscious onto the page. It's easy to look back now and say it followed from A to zed, but don't forget, I was also trying to be a Yank during a lot of this time, from Princeton, '54 to the Stanford University School of Business.

I actually was accepted at Stanford Business School. I had applied to keep my mother off my back; she was one of the many to see I had no negotiable skills, and maybe two years at business school would shape me up. I so hated the idea of Stanford Business School that I volunteered for the army. I ask you to consider me as a draftee—a middle-class Irish Catholic with a stutter, an undistinguished history degree from Princeton, the politics of an alderman, and social graces polished to a high gloss at the Hartford Gold Club. What I wanted most in life was to be an Episcopalian. What I became was a PFC in a gun battery in Germany.

As educations go, Baker Battery was as good as any I had received at boarding school or at Princeton. The battery commander was a drunk, the first sergeant had syphilis, and the medic was what we used to call in those days "queer." I shared a room in the barracks with the medic and his twin, a cannoneer in the gun section whose elevator did not go all the way to the top floor. In the room next door there were a couple of brothers from Tennessee. Their last name was Jethro. Neither had a first name. The older brother was W. X. Jethro, the younger Y. Z. Jethro. The army to me was like a Rhodes scholarship.

In retrospect, I have made a living off the army for the past forty years. It was my passport out of the stalag of the middle class into the terra incognita of the culturally and economically stateless. The army helped define a voice, the same way that parochial school did, the way that insane desire to be assimilated did, and as did the tension between the gutter Irish parochial schoolboy and the cloned Yank in white tie and tails at the Hartford debutante parties.

The voice defined an attitude, an attitude toward life and toward material. Let me say something here that will come as somewhat surprising to those of you who are not writers. Writers are always being approached by people who say, "I've got this terrific story to tell, if only I had the time to tell it...."

In a word, *bullshit*. There are no good stories. There is only an attitude toward the story. And that attitude is defined by all those things I mentioned earlier—the wound stripes of life.

Let me give you Henry James. Here he is on this rather crucial subject:

The power to guess the unseen from the seen, to trace the implications of things, to judge the whole piece by the pattern, the condition of feeling life in general so completely that you are well on your way to knowing any particular corner of it—this cluster of gifts may also be said to constitute experience . . . if experience consists of impressions, it may [also] be said that impressions are experience.

So, James concludes, write from experience, of course, but experience as he defines it. And most important: "try to be one of the people on whom nothing is lost."

Try to be one of the people on whom nothing is lost. For a writer that single sentence is like the Sermon on the Mount.

Let's go back to particular voices, the voices of a few writers I know, or knew, on whom nothing is, or was, ever lost. Writers with individual voices, writers with an attitude framed by the lives they have led, and the backgrounds they came from. The writers are Jimmy Breslin, Tom Wolfe, Barry Farrell, and Calvin Trillin.

Jimmy first, because he is a mick malcontent like me. Jimmy has the voice of a New York that most of you will never see. It is not a J-school voice, and he covers venues most reporters today stay away from. He's a reporter the way that other people of his generation were firemen or policemen. It was a trade. He is fast, funny, abusive; he gives you a scato-logical guided tour of those members of society with 24-inch necks and 56-inch waists, people whose pictures usually appear in the papers with raincoats hiding their faces or with their names spelled in plastic letters on an NYPD mug shot, full face, left and right profile. He is the last of a New York breed: a five-borough pavement pounder who never learned how to drive because in a car you can't talk to the guy on the street and learn about his wife's bunions and his brother's parole hearing. Not driving gives Jimmy an attitude. Actually, it just adds to the consider-able attitude he was born with. He's a public transportation, MTA, taxi commission reporter. He took a cab to the riots in Crown Heights and got his skull broken. He doesn't go to the country. Or he might go, but he never spends the night.

He brings city wisdom even to international affairs. Recently he was talking about the $25 million reward the administration was offering for anyone who would snitch out Osama bin Laden. And he said that even if Osama bin Laden were handed over on a platter tomorrow, the snitch would never get the $25 million from the man he always calls "Bush the President."

That's a little jab he gives everyone. No first names, just last name and job title. As in Navasky the professor. It's something to remember. Anyway, this is Jimmy on Bush the President's reward and how you stiff whoever claims it:

> There was one day when this David Berkowitz, or "Son of Sam," was running around killing young women and Frank McLoughlin, then with the police, was telling Mike O'Neill, the editor of the *Daily News*, to put up a reward.
>
> "Ten thousand," O'Neill said.
>
> "Make it a hundred thousand," McLoughlin said.
>
> O'Neill said, "I can't just put up an amount like that without a conference."
>
> McLoughlin said, "Announce the hundred. In the history of the city nobody ever paid a reward. They have to be caught, indicted, found guilty and then get through an appeal before the person who turned the guy in can ask for the money. Then what you tell him, that's fine, but you really didn't convict him. Twelve jurors did that. So you pay nothing."

With Jimmy, they broke the mold. He still has copycats, but there is Breslin and there is School of Breslin. Stick with the original.

Then there's Tom Wolfe. As different from Jimmy as night from day, but his voice is just as distinctive.

The clues to a culture are in its style, and Tom has always been a creature of style. As if to make this point unavoidable, he took unto himself a style. There were the white suit and the white socks with clocks and the hat that looked as if it had been lifted from the head of a Marseille gangster. There was the complexion as pale as a loaf of stale Wonder bread. In fact, he looked like nothing so much as a male Edith Sitwell. He used language not to explain but to distort, to create an illusion, a kind of verbal impressionism, each paragraph a funhouse mirror. "At about the age of thirteen, as I recall," he said at the Hopwood Lecture he gave at the

University of Michigan, "I became intrigued by words that began with J. They looked marvelous to me. 'Jaded.' 'Jejune.' I didn't even know how to pronounce 'jejune'; in fact, to this day I have never heard anyone use the word in conversation, but I put it in every chance I had. . . . Pretty soon it became a noun as well as an adjective. 'The jaded jejune of his hopes,' that sort of thing, and finally it became a verb as well. People were jejuning each other all over the place."

Worse yet, this parvenu refused to be a recipient of received wisdom, another clone of the liberal consensus. Tom is a Southerner not burdened by his Southernness, a Southerner who did not wish, as Elizabeth Hardwick, another great Southerner, once said she wished, to become a New York Jewish intellectual. The New York Jewish intellectual, however, did not escape Tom's attention, and he was not above doing a little jejuning about the New York Jewish intellectual's habitat. "His is an apartment of a sort known as West Side Married Intellectual," he wrote in *Mauve Gloves & Madmen, Clutter & Vine*. "The rooms are big, the layout is good, but the moldings, cornices, covings, and chair rails seem to be corroding. Actually they are merely lumpy from too many coats of paint over the decades, and the parquet sections of the floor have dried out and are sprung loose from one another. . . . The building has a doorman but no elevator man, and on Sundays the door is manned by a janitor in gray khaki work clothes."

With that same cold eye, Tom fastened on the new elites of the social frontier. Whatever the endeavor out there on the social ne plus ultra, there were those who did it better, who had the right stuff, the ineffable quality of excellence. Always he was interested in why the cream rose to the top. That the stuff may have curdled and soured was of little interest to him. He was an anthropologist who had not lost faith in his method. The tensile strength of molybdenum and the color of the copy paper at *The New Yorker* were for him of equal importance. "Why did things work?" That is always Tom's question.

And now Trillin. I've known Bud for forty years. My wife and I are the only two people who call him Calvin, mainly because we think it's funny that a Kansas City Jew is named after John Calvin.

Bud and I were at *Time* together. We arrived at more or less the same time, and we left at more or less the same time, as indeed did John McPhee and Barry Farrell. I don't mind saying that I think the four of us were pretty good.

A quick sidebar here about Barry Farrell. Barry is probably not known to you because he died young; he was not fifty when he was simultaneously hit by a stroke and a massive heart attack while he was driving in L.A., but he was as talented as any journalist of my generation.

He was that rare writer who looked the way a writer should look, tall, jug-eared, bearded, sandy-haired. I remember once seeing him standing at the elevator at *Time*, wearing a trench coat and smoking a Gauloise (another wonderful affect, as was the occasional joint he would sometimes puff while in conference with the managing editor, confident in that innocent time that the editor would think it only some particularly noisome foreign tobacco he had picked up on his travels).

He was stylish, but there was so much substance beneath the style. Those eyes, the voice—Barry was that rare person who talked in complete sentences, every sentence perfectly parsed, plural predicates for plural subjects, no dangling participles, every clause modifying what it was supposed to modify, "that" never confused with "which"—people trusted him, they told him things they would never tell another reporter. He liked cops and coroners and city hall bureaucrats, and to him they would confide the most appalling tales of municipal mendacity. Barry was a great chronicler of the city, any city; he understood the internal rhyming scheme of city hall meetings and committee reports, finding in the impenetrable diction of officialdom the broken meters that concealed collusion and fraud.

He was a tenacious questioner, never deflected, following a kind of quiet Jesuitical logic, a holdover from the Catholicism he had long since abandoned, one that allowed him to illuminate dark corners. "Is Gary well hung?" he suddenly asked a jailhouse snitch about the stoolie's former cellmate, Gary Gilmore; it was a startling question, posed without judgment, perfectly evoking a world without women where any member, any orifice might offer opportunity for sexual release. Prison aristocracies intrigued him; "bum bandit" was the term he coined for a cell-block sexual imperialist, and he studied the bum bandits and the punks and all the subcategories in between with the eye of an anthropologist.

Happiness for Barry was a motel on the Utah sand flats, interviewing Gary Gilmore on Death Row through a filter of lawyers; it was the obstacle that obsessed him, and the adrenalin and the ingenuity needed to overcome it, and if his Gilmore interviews only provided the subsoil out of which grew Norman Mailer's *The Executioner's Song,* what the hell, he would get back to his own work later. This was a moment in history not to be missed. Mailer had him pegged. "Someone was always dying in his stories," Norman wrote in *The Executioner's Song.*

> Oscar Bonavena getting killed, Bobby Hall, young blond girls getting offed on highways in California. One cult slaying or another. He even had the reputation of being good at it. His telephone number leaped to the mind of various editors. Barry Farrell, crime reporter, with an inner life exasperatingly Catholic. Led his life out of his financial and emotional exigencies, took the jobs his bills and his battered psyche required him to take, but somehow his assignments always took him into some great new moral complexity. Got into his writing like a haze.

Remember I said earlier that writing is a license to be curious. You went to Barry and Marcia's house in Hollywood for dinner and there was a little dope and a lot of booze and there were actors and NBA basketball players and writers and defendants and vice cops and lawyers and every kind of loony toon. I remember one sweet old woman with a wooden leg who designed turn-on clothes for the hookers who worked the legal Nevada whorehouses, outfits with little heart-shaped openings framing the pubic symphysis. "Symphysis" is one of those words like "jejune" was for Tom Wolfe. I'm not quite sure what it means, but I love it.

Another quick detour, about *Time* during the late '50s and early '60s. It was a glorious place to hang out in those years. I was 27 when I was hired, an ignoramus, vintage Princeton '54. I got my job because a woman I was seeing on the sly, Vassar '57, was also seeing George J.W. Goodman, Harvard '52, a writer in *Time*'s business section who was later to become the author and PBS economics guru "Adam Smith." Jerry Goodman, I was informed by Vassar '57, was leaving *Time* for *Fortune*, which meant that if I moved fast there was probably a job open. I applied to *Time*'s personnel man, a friend, Yale '49, and was in due course interviewed by Otto Fuerbringer, Harvard '32, and *Time*'s managing editor. The cut of my orange and black jib seemed to satisfy him, and the $7,700 a year I was offered more than satisfied me, and so a few weeks later I went to work as a writer in the business section, although I was not altogether certain about the difference between a stock and a bond, and had no clue what "over the counter" meant.

The *Time* of those years was pervaded by a kind of Protestant entitlement (no matter that I was an Irish Catholic; I felt spiritually brevetted a Protestant), and equally as important, the arrogance that went with it, an arrogance often spectacularly unearned (as in my case), or earned largely in the city rooms of the *Harvard Crimson* or the *Yale Daily News* or the *Daily Princetonian* or, occasionally, the *Columbia Spectator*. A corporate hubris prevailed, a confidence in ourselves and in our place in the world. However misplaced this confidence, there was a verbal esprit de corps, a sense of purpose founded on the conviction that every Tuesday *Time* would give the educated man (the educated woman was considered so minor a factor that the magazine would not hire women writers; women on the staff could only aspire to be researchers, the *Time* equivalent of domestics) a review of the previous week's events presented with a political rigor and an intellectual brio. There was no namby-pamby objectivity; *Time* had a partisan Republican point of view, and if it was one not shared by many of its gentrified Ivy Leaguers, few felt the compulsion to quit. The excessive compression of the week's news led to what became known as *Time* style, often ludicrous, easily parodied, but rich with possibilities for veiled and not so veiled innuendo.

We were amateurs for the most part, inspired amateurs in some cases, discoursing easily on the brushstrokes and color schemes of Bernard Buffet one week and on the financial restructuring of the Malaysian economy planned by Tunku Abdul Rahman the next, and few were ever the wiser.

Calvin and John and Barry and I did not learn how to write at *Time*. What we learned was to write fast and to make deadlines. Then when we had mined it for all we could, we all left. I don't even read *Time* on planes anymore, but like the army, I don't begrudge a moment I spent there.

Now Calvin's voice: he is best known as a humorist, but his America is informed more by Sherwood Anderson than by Garrison Keillor; he is attracted to stories about people who behave, if not exactly badly, then certainly not well, with the result that many of his pieces, especially when they are read one after another (as in his book *Killings*), appear to be drawn from a deeply conservative reserve that seems at times almost melancholic. The prose is spare and unadorned, like a tree in late autumn stripped of its leaves; it is without ego—in his reporting the pronoun "I" almost never appears—and without tricks. Of course, making it seem without tricks is the biggest trick of all.

The pertinent detail in the social weave never escapes him. "'It's a matter of honor with an Italian hit man not to touch anything,'" he quotes a homicide detective saying on the subject of murder. "'Cubans rob the guy as part of the deal—the price plus what he's carrying.'" His tone is usually conversational, at times seeming to come almost from an oral tradition. He begins a piece about a Louisiana woman's fight with a lawyer in a state agency over whether her parents should have been identified as "white" or "colored" on her birth certificate in this deceptively simple way: "Susie Guillory Phipps thinks this all started in 1977, when she wanted to apply for a passport. Jack Westholtz thinks it started long before that."

Like Murray Kempton, Calvin—Bud—tries to find something good to say, however recherché, about those who have violated every clause of the human contract. "Even people who assume all criminal lawyers to be part fixer," he wrote of a high-flying, seven-times-married Miami Beach criminal attorney found shot to death in his car, "refer to Harvey St. Jean as a gentleman." And of a lupine music promoter: "Morris Levy was a seventh-grade dropout from the Bronx who became one of the most powerful figures in the record business. . . . He was a friend, and occasionally a business partner of mobsters; he was also a Man of the Year at United Jewish Appeal dinners, and a planter of forests in Israel."

The ludicrous holds particular appeal. The late Harvey St. Jean, he wrote, had lived at a private club "where the average age of the residents was forty," and then he added the local computation of that average: " 'a sixty-year-old guy and a twenty-year-old broad.' "

At a certain point in your professional life, a certain kind of people interest you, a certain kind of situation, a situation that you sense is a little more complicated than it appears on the face of it. Harvey St. Jean. Morris Levy.

That is why writers are so drawn to convicts. Convicts inhabit a perfectly ordered world of the illegal, the illicit, and the violent, a world that could be said to have a constitution all its own. I used to have a correspondence with a con called Eddie. He wrote me a letter and the return address said, "SPSM—State Prison of Southern Michigan. World's Largest Walled Prison. Better known as the Walled-Off Astoria." I was hooked.

With every letter he would send me copies of *The Spectator*—"The World's Largest Prison Weekly—7500 Copies Circulated Weekly," as the banner put it. "Lot of crap in it," Eddie wrote, "but the prison white-collars eat it up. Looks good in the reports, and a guy can make a special out of here on it."

I read *The Spectator* avidly. One feature was called "The Quarter Century Club," which was profiles of convicts who had spent twenty-five or more continuous years in prison.

Here's an entry about one quarter-century dubber: "After 33 years behind prison bars, JoJo today is a slow-walking, stoop-shouldered individual who has felt the weight of these many years of disillusionment, disappointment, discouragement, and most of all, distrust for others."

Not bad, all that alliteration. You notice, however, that there is no mention of why JoJo had been in the slam for those thirty-three years. As a matter of fact, *The Spectator* never mentioned why any inmate was doing time, just the length of his sentence and the county where the sentence was pronounced. It was like he was at Andover, or Hotchkiss.

There were also some wonderful social notes: "Prison is a most unusual place for a family to get together," one of them said, "but down through the years, SPSM has had its share of relatives doing time together. Therefore the brothers Bob and Billy Buick are no oddity. The exceptional thing about the Buick brothers is a sparkling personality that will attract most everyone they encounter. Cap this with their excellent ability to get along with people, and you have their key to doing time. . . ."

Gold.

It was almost a year before Eddie got around to telling me why he was inside. He slipped it in, almost parenthetically, in the middle of what amounted to his autobiography. He had left the navy, and his wife had divorced him. "Well, by now I'm too old to go back and finish my twenty years," he wrote. "Well, I run the country for a while and gets married again, that lasts about a hot minute, and I'm in the joint because I offt her. But still, it's not worth it, but what else could I have done, the way things were." How things were remained unspecified, but apparently bad enough to impel him to off Mrs. Eddie. He then went on to tell me where I could send a Christmas package or a money order, were I so disposed. Our correspondence ended shortly thereafter.

You might not ever use it. But it adds to the attitude, and it is the attitude and the replenishment of knowledge, as I have too often said this evening, that gives you the voice. You want to keep on adding to the attitude. You do that in a lot of ways.

Read a lot of poetry. Auden, say. Or Gerard Manley Hopkins. Why? Because it helps you punctuate. It is a recurring cliché now that if anyone writes about September 11, she or he has to trot out some lines from Auden's "September 1, 1939."

> I sit in one of the dives
> On Fifty-second Street
> Uncertain and afraid
> As the clever hopes expire
> Of a low dishonest decade . . .

Recently I did a long piece for *The New York Review of Books* about the Okinawa campaign at the end of the Pacific War, the last and bloodiest battle of World War II, and I was trying to explain the paralyzing fear felt by the Marines on the island, and the sense that they were not going to live through the next minute, that they had been reduced, as I said in the piece, "physically and emotionally . . . to a near zombie state."

"One is reminded," I wrote, "of Gerard Manley Hopkins: 'I wake and feel the fell of dark, not day.'"

And also read the oddball stuff. I read trade magazines and catalogs; they're the only publications I subscribe to. *American Lawyer, Shotgun News, The Trident*—that's the publication of Delta Delta Delta, my wife's sorority. Katie Couric, Catherine Crier, and Elizabeth Dole, Tri-Delts all. If you want a handle on the middle-class American woman, look at *The Trident. Soldier of Fortune* used to be a gold mine of gun lore, a Bible of violence. In its pages, I noted how to kill a man with a pistol, preferably an H&K P9S 45 cal. ACP, with a polygon barrel for increased accuracy. You don't shoot the target in the head. That assumes that all parts of the head are equal. "The objective is a no-reflex kill." The objective therefore is to cut the medulla oblongata. The medulla oblongata is the widening of the spinal cord at the base of the brain. If you're aiming low, the motor nerves in the pelvic girdle will bring a target down. It is the particularity of the pelvic girdle and the medulla oblongata that I find of interest. I suppose in the last thirty years I've used the phrases "medulla oblongata" or "pelvic girdle" in various pieces three or four times. If it's there, use it.

I'd like to go back to something I said earlier. If you do magazine journalism, I said, "why" ultimately matters as much as or even more than "who," "what," "where," "when," and "how." And not so much "why" as a meditation on "why." Or a contemplation on "how" or "who." A benefit of age is that you are allowed to contemplate. Or meditate. Or both.

I'd like to give an example, from a piece I wrote about the O. J. Simpson case for *The New York Review*. It was done before the trial, before jury selection, before Johnnie Cochran was even involved. I wrote it because I thought most of the stuff I read was bullshit, easy and sentimental takes about the principals, and about the West Side of Los Angeles. We had lived a block or so from the Simpsons in Brentwood during our last years in L.A., and we'd never met them, but I would see them at the Country Mart or driving or jogging. They'd already entered the national mythology, and I thought the mythology, especially in the *Times* and

Newsweek, was received and secondhand, so I wanted to it look at it from another angle. Here it is. First O. J.:

> The life of the professional athlete is an unreal, emotionally under-developed existence, lived at the frontier of instinct and reflex, where the difference between success and failure can be measured in microseconds; split vision, muscle memory, and hand-to-eye coordination are better refined than the vocabulary to explain them. That the athlete will never again do anything in his life as well as what he does at age twenty-five is a truth best left unstated. As long as he can perform, the athlete has an exemption from the realities of life; his physical skills will endure, and his every whim is a demand likely to be satisfied.
>
> Sexual entitlement is a part of the package, as if the women who are drawn to him and his fame and his riches are just another bonus clause in his contract, a perk, like the suite on the road and the free rental car at his disposal. By the time he is thirty, he is professionally in decline, especially if, like O. J. Simpson, he is a running back with chancy knees. After sports, if he still manages to maintain his high profile, he is really famous for formerly being famous. It is a constantly diminishing psychic bank account on which to draw. He is too old to begin the kind of work that promises much reward, even if he were educated, qualified, and so disposed. Sports broadcasting and television huckstering allow some of the better-known to trade on their names for a few more years, until a newer, fresher retiree appears. For other semi-solvent former stars, retirement becomes an endless treadmill of card shows, fantasy camps, celebrity golf tournaments, old timers' games, and meet-and-greet paid appearances at the weddings, birthdays, anniversaries, and bar mitzvahs of strangers, every handshake rung up on a cash register, the sexual favor provided by the randy guest in the nature of a tip.
>
> O. J. Simpson was one of the few retired athletes, and certainly the first black, able to exploit his retirement, becoming in the process more widely known than he ever was as a football player,

known to a generation that had never seen him on a gridiron, a favorite of women as well as men who fantasized their own eighty-yard runs. He was the quintessential intimate stranger, the person we think we know because of his celebrity. Surrounding him was the sort of entourage that regularly attaches itself to superannuated former athletes, rich white sports fanatics basking in the reflected warmth of his fame as he basked in the comfort of their wealth, and the kind of celebrity lawyers who like to hang with the celebrities they represent, sharing in the overflow of drugs and girls. The entourage became to Simpson in retirement what the Electric Company, his offensive line in Buffalo, had been in his playing days, protectors of the franchise, middle-aged schmoozers and hangers-on shielding the Juice from any bad news, letting him go on thinking, as he had his entire life, that should trouble ever arrive it could be handled.

Then Ron Goldman:

The late film director Sam Peckinpah once told me that the only Hollywood story worth making was one he called "The Third Man Through the Door." There is the star, Peckinpah said, there's the star's consort, and then there's the third man through the door, holding it open for the other two, the one whose face is blurred out in the publicity photographs. Ronald Lyle Goldman seemed the definition of the third man through the door. He was twenty-five, a college dropout from Illinois, his looks as gorgeously unexceptional as Nicole Brown Simpson's. What he wanted was never quite clear. He modeled once for Armani, he gave tennis lessons, he worked out on the machines at The Gym, and he waited tables at Mezzaluna, a crummy second-rate Brentwood restaurant elevated in the post-murder stories in *The New York Times* to a "hot spot." Sometimes he told friends he wanted to own a restaurant of his own, other times that if he had not "made it" (making it at what never precisely defined) by thirty, he would like to become a paramedic. It was a life not unpleasurably adrift, and so it might have remained, had Ronald Lyle Goldman not had the misfortune to meet Nicole Brown Simpson.

Finally Nicole Brown:

At 33, Nicole Brown Simpson was essentially returning to the life she was leading when she met her ex-husband sixteen years earlier, except that now she had a white Ferrari with the kind of vanity license plate that adolescents favor—L84AD8, or Late For A Date.

Nicole Brown was scarcely more than a child herself when she met O. J. Simpson. She was seventeen, a homecoming princess at Dana Hills High School in the Orange County beach community of Monarch Point. Higher education was not an option she vigorously pursued. Tall and willowy, she worked as a boutique sales clerk, and then as a waitress at the Daisy, a Beverly Hills private disco; and it was there that O. J. Simpson, thirty years old, shakily married to his first wife, his football career just about over, fixed on Nicole Brown.

It is perhaps useful here to pause and consider the kind of young woman still in her teens who becomes the consort of a high-profile swinger half a generation older. What the child women who make this choice bring with them is youth, a compliant disposition, a taste for the world's goods, and a minimal sense of their own identity. They are defined by the men they sleep with; sex is their primary vocabulary. [We learned later via her "friends" and "supporters" that Nicole Brown was a woman with breast implants, a talent for fellatio, an appreciation of a prominent phallus, and a taste for controlled substances.] She had a personal trainer, a nutritionist, a fully staffed household, two children, an apartment on Manhattan's East Side, an oceanfront vacation house in Laguna Beach, holidays in Hawaii and Mexico, and skiing trips to Colorado. In actuality, however, she was chattel with a wedding ring, her security a 911 emergency number she had good occasion to call often.

In the neighborhood of San Vicente Boulevard, to which she gravitated with her children Sydney and Justin after the divorce,

Nicole Brown Simpson still had the cachet of her married name. Being close to her was as close as any of her new friends in this habitat of the young, the tan, and the beautiful would probably ever get to fame. She jogged under the coral trees on the San Vicente median, turned up at The Gym and Starbuck's, and oversaw the after-school activities of her children. She tooled around Brentwood in her Ferrari, sometimes letting Ron Goldman drive it, and at night she danced in local clubs. Friends said she was enjoying her freedom, becoming her own woman.

A black ex-athlete growing older ungracefully, tenuously living a white life on the limited visa of his contract as a television pitchman; his beautiful battered ex-wife trying at age thirty-five to start over and make her own way after a half a lifetime on someone else's tab; a waiter and unsuccessful male model uncertain whether to become a restaurateur or a paramedic, collecting business cards from the men on whose tables he waited in case one might decide to invest in his dream restaurant: these were characters of considerable and ambiguous particularity. With the events of June 12, however, when Nicole Brown Simpson and Ronald Lyle Goldman were found slashed and stabbed to death, and with the arrest of Orenthal James Simpson for killing them, all three lost whatever identity they had in the frantic search to find some larger meaning that would explain the crime. The story demanded a moral: youth wasted, promise denied, spousal abuse, domestic violence, the race card. "Show me a hero," Scott Fitzgerald once jotted in his notebooks, "and I will write you a tragedy."

And one last contemplation. Or meditation. I assume that many of you saw the movie *Boys Don't Cry,* which won Hillary Swank an Oscar for her performance as Teena Brandon, the gender-ambivalent young woman who tried to pass herself off as a male lothario in the rural Nebraska town of Falls City, and wound up getting herself and two other people murdered on New Year's Eve 1994. I found the movie effective and affecting, but it did play fast and loose with the facts. I had written about the case in *The New Yorker* in 1997, visiting Falls City four times over the course of three years. Without disparaging the movie, I thought the case less about gender than about class, and so I would like to read you part of that piece:

> Violence is the way stupid people try to level the playing field. Tom Nissen and John Lotter, John Lotter and Tom Nissen: their sociopathic curricula vitae were so similar as to be interchangeable. Psychiatric instability, tumultuous family lives, absentee fathers, trigger tempers, suicidal tendencies, foster homes, runaway living, a fascination with lethal objects, juvenile detention, sexual promiscuity, deficient IQs, aversion to education, substance abuse, crime (theft and burglary for Lotter, arson for Nissen), prison. Hyperactive and a slow learner, John Lotter would use whatever weapon he could lay his hands on—hammer, pencil, knife—to beat up and injure other children. When he was nine, a juvenile court declared him "uncontrollable," and he became a ward of the state; he was, in fact, so uncontrollable that he was turned down by Boys Town, which seemed to disprove Father Edward Flanagan's piety that there was no such thing as a bad boy. The only person who could get through to him was Lana Tisdel, a local femme fatale with a fitful sex drive who had known him since they were children, and with whom he maintained an off and on relationship between incarcerations.
>
> Nissen's mother, Sharon, had her first child (out of wedlock) when she was 14, and married Nissen's father, Ed, after a ten-day courtship when she was 15 (Ed Nissen was not the father of Sharon's oldest child); when his parents split, Nissen, then 4, moved to Mississippi with his father. As he advanced into adolescence, he began stealing cars (including an 18-wheeler), flirted with white supremacy, and finally moved back to Falls City with his mother, who was now married to an ex-con and carrying a full rap sheet of her own—bad checks, DWI, resisting arrest. Nissen ran off to a homeless shelter in Washington state, enlisted in the army, went over the hill, and traveled with a carnival before returning to Nebraska, where he landed in the arms of Kandi Gibson, a sixteen-year-old unmarried mother with a six-month-old daughter. In

June 1992, Nissen and Kandi married; a few days later Nissen cheated on his wife with one of her friends. He also had a violent altercation with a male friend he claimed was flashing a photograph around Falls City of Kandi fellating an acquaintance. Twenty days after his marriage, Nissen was arrested for setting two fires in Falls City; in September 1992, he was convicted of second degree arson, and received a sentence of one to three years in prison.

The penitentiary offered Lotter and Nissen the only structured environment they had ever really experienced. Survival in prison is predicated on a simple premise: power rules. Sexual imperialism flourishes; in a world of men without women, the weak belong to the strong. According to someone who had done time with him, Lotter attracted the attention of a convict with the discomforting nickname of "Tugboat." In the predicament in which they found themselves after Teena Brandon's interrogation by Sheriff Laux, Lotter and Nissen reverted to the penitentiary premise. If they had been powerless in prison, here was a situation where they thought they had the power. They had both done hard time, they did not want to go back to prison, and they thought Teena Brandon could make a rape charge stick. Having threatened to kill her if she talked, it was as if they thought a failure to carry through on that threat would be considered less than manly.

Logic seemed a missing chromosome. Rape is historically difficult to prosecute, and county sheriffs and small town police in rural jurisdictions are often less than diligent in the pursuit of the accused, good old boys who will invariably argue that the sex was consensual. As of June 1996, no rape case had come to trial in Richardson County in the fifteen years that the clerk of the district court had been on the job. Charges are usually dropped, generally when the alleged victim refuses to testify, as Teena Brandon, whose history was to cut and run in the face of trouble, might well have done. Rape is a crime, moreover, that rarely has witnesses; if charges are brought, the case usually degenerates into a disputatious litany of *he said, she said*. That a jury was unlikely to convict Lotter and Nissen of rape, especially given Teena Brandon's gender ambiguity, was a factor they seemed never to consider. With demented con cunning, they thought murder was the only way they could evade the rape charge, that a dead witness could not testify. What they also failed to consider was that murder, under the circumstances, would be far easier to prove than rape, and that if the putative rape victim was killed, they would be the top suspects.

Shortly after midnight on December 31, 1993, their inchoate rage inflamed by a five-day drunk, Lotter and Nissen finally worked up the nerve to act.

Question to Thomas Nissen from the special prosecutor: "As you drove to Humboldt from Falls City that night, was there any discussion along the way of what was going to happen once you got there?"

Answer from Thomas Nissen: "Me and John Lotter talked about killing Teena Brandon, and I told John Lotter . . . that if he shot Teena Brandon and there was other people around, that the other people would have to be killed also."

Five minutes in the farmhouse, three people dead. Nissen and Lotter drove into Kansas on the way home, so as to approach Falls City from the south rather than from the north; if they were spotted, they would be seen coming not from Humboldt but from the opposite direction—con cunning again. On the outskirts of Falls City, they stopped and threw a box containing the gloves, the handgun, and the knife into the Nemeha River. The river, however, was frozen, and the box remained on the ice, where investigators found it the next day after the bodies were discovered at Lisa Lambert's house, and the alarm went out to pick up Nissen and Lotter, the most viable suspects. The knife was in a sheath, and on the sheath was marked the owner's name—LOTTER.

On winter roads, the 26-mile drive from Falls City to Humboldt takes 31 minutes. Over the course of that half hour, rational people might assume that the fevers of vengeance would subside. Except for a contract Mafia hit of *The Godfather* variety or a territorial firefight among drug dealers, criminals do not deliberately embark on a mission they know will result in multiple murders. At some point, self-preservation would kick in, and with it the sure understanding that the killing of three people would increase the penalties exponentially. With Nissen and Lotter, there seemed an almost delusionary disengagement from reality. They were like the characters in Oliver Stone's *Natural Born Killers,* high on doing it. I kept trying to imagine the scene when they left the farmhouse, wondering what ran through their minds after executing three people. There was no escape, no place to run. They must have known they would have been the first suspects, but they made no attempt to flee. They both had grown up in Nebraska, knew the bitter cold of the Nebraska winter, knew that the rivers and their tributaries froze, but still they threw their weapons onto the ice-covered Nemeha, I can only think, since they seemed to have no other reference than the movies, because killers in gangster pictures throw their guns into the river after committing murder. Their single alibi attempt was to order Kandi Nissen and Rhonda McKensie to lie if asked what time the two returned to Nissen's house—one p.m. was the time they agreed on. Then they went to sleep, Rhonda and Lotter on the floor in Nissen's living room, Nissen and Kandi in their bedroom. I wondered if they had sex, one last spasmatic release before investigators came the next day to arrest them and return them to a world where Tugboat was sovereign.

"If you can't get laid in Falls City, you have a serious problem," Thomas Nissen wrote me from the Lincoln Correctional Center in the summer of 1995. To clear up any misunderstanding he thought I might have about his attitude toward Teena Brandon's sexual prevarication, he said in another letter: "I hate, and am totally against homosexuality between men. Between men is sick. Between women, it's such a show of love. I think it's cool." About Falls City: "Lots of alcohol and seldom a shortage of drugs. Most of the time the county jail is full. Not much for the younger race to do but drink, drive, and dodge the boys in blue. Lots of unmarried moms and kids. There is very little work to be found. Even when there is work, it doesn't last for long. . . . Good things do come out of Richardson County. If I ever hear of one, I'll be sure to tell you. That was a joke."

In one of my letters, I asked Nissen if he ever contemplated the element of chance that had put five such disparate people together in the Humboldt farmhouse the night of the murders. Nissen replied immediately.

"A million ifs," he wrote. "What if I had never went to the bar in November and met the Tisdels. What if I had simply been faithful to my wife, or not drank, or not allowed Brandon to live in my home, or bailed him out of jail, or liked him, or not even cared. Had I not been fucking other women, I never would have met Lotter when I did. After all, Rhonda McKensie would have not been staying at my home had I not left Kandi alone for so many damn lonely nights. What if Brandon had been honest, or told everyone the truth when push come to shove. What if on Dec. 23, Brandon had told me, Tom, I'm really a girl and please take me home because I think I might get hurt. What if Brandon would have ran when the car got stuck on the late night of the 24 of December [the night of the rape]. He had the chance. What if I had recked [*sic*] the car like I thought of doing on the way to Lisa's home, or what if there had been a gun in Lisa's house, or what if Phil had not got into a fight with Leslie, or Missy been awake when I was at Lana's home on the early hours of the 31st, or if Brandon had been put in jail when we took him to court in Lincoln, or I had been busted on a dirty U.A. [urinalysis] while on parole, or if I had listened to Kandi when she told me not to have nothing to do with Lana, if I had killed myself, or if the gun had never been fixed, or if I had simply said, No. The list could go on and on. Yes, sir, fate can be a motherfucker."

I've been doing this for over forty years, and "Yes, sir, fate can be a motherfucker" is the single best line a subject ever gave me.

2

Magazine Editing Then and Now

Ruth Reichl, an author, journalist, and chef, served as the editor-in-chief of *Gourmet* magazine from 1999 until the magazine's closure in 2009. Her books include *Tender at the Bone: Growing Up at the Table* (1998), *Comfort Me with Apples: More Adventures at the Table* (2001), and *Garlic and Sapphires: The Secret Life of a Critic in Disguise* (2005). She was the restaurant critic for *New West* magazine, the *Los Angeles Times* restaurant critic and food editor, and *The New York Times* restaurant critic. Reichl compiled and contributed chapters to *Endless Feasts: 60 Years of Writing for Gourmet* (2002) and *The Gourmet Cookbook* (2004). Her first lecture was on April 4, 2003 and the second was delivered on February 26, 2009.

I thought I would maybe start by telling you a little bit about my background, and how I ended up here.

I was cooking at a small restaurant in Berkeley, California, in the mid-'70s, when an editor of *New West* magazine—which was a magazine that Clay Felker started as the sister publication of *New York* magazine—sent me off to write my first restaurant review.

Now, I have to set the scene for you here: my husband and I are living in a commune in Berkeley. We have no money. I mean, we have not been to a restaurant in years. We were literally living on nothing. And there are eight of us in the household. And the notion that I was going to take all of my friends out for a free meal was unbelievably exciting to us. And everybody went off to Value Village, the thrift store, to get clothes to wear for this event. I didn't have a credit card. The only car I had was a Volvo, which started with a screwdriver and which, of course, I couldn't give to a valet.

So we all gather in the hall of the house and we are going to go to this restaurant called Robert. It is the fanciest French restaurant in San Francisco. We climb into my husband's van. Doug is an artist, and he was working with light, and he had turned his van into a moving *camera obscura*. So it had no windows. But he had painted the inside white and he had put a wooden partition right behind the driver's seat and put mattresses on the floor, and made a little pinhole in the partition. So when you lay on the floor, you could see the landscape projected upside down onto the walls of the van.

So we all—in our thrift-store clothes—lie down on the floor of this van and we drive across the San Francisco Bay Bridge to San Francisco. And, of course, we park around the corner because we don't want anyone to see us getting out of this disreputable van. And we go into this restaurant.

Now, my friends all are very excited about the possibility that I might get this job permanently. And they all decide that they're going to be very helpful. I later learned—in my many years as a restaurant critic— that the last thing you want is anybody to be helpful. You just want to take people to eat the meal and be quiet about it while you are making the judgments. But I didn't know that at the time.

So each of them appoints himself a different thing to pay attention to. One is watching the waiters and the tables around us. And the best cook in the group is sitting there going, "Yes, I think there's thyme in here, and a little white wine and shallot." And the wine expert in the group is paying attention to every nuance of the wine list.

And as I am watching them all trying so hard to be helpful, I have one of these epiphanies that, if you're very lucky, every once in a while you get as a writer: I see us as a gang that has been sent by a rival restaurateur to find fault with this restaurant. And I rush home and, in a blaze of inspiration, I write this piece that I call, "Cops and Roberts." It is essentially a little noir short story, and it starts, "The names have all been changed to protect the innocent." And I spin out this story and I weave the food into it. But it is anything but a traditional restaurant review.

And the next day, I drive back to San Francisco and throw it on my editor's desk. And—because I couldn't find a place to park and couldn't afford a parking lot—I run back downstairs and get back in the car and drive back across the Bay Bridge. And as I'm driving across the bridge, the stupidity of what I have just done hits me. And I say, "That wasn't a restaurant review, it was a short story. It wasn't even a very good short story. You've just thrown this great job away." And I see myself back at the restaurant forever. *I'm never going to be a restaurant critic. None of my friends are ever going to talk to me because I've blown this job.*

And the minute that I can, I get off the freeway and I run—this is, of course, before cell phones—so I run to the first phone booth I can find and I throw some quarters in and I call my editor. And I say, "Jon, Jon, don't read that piece. I picked up the wrong one. I don't know what made me do that. I'm on my way home. I'm going to bring the right piece back. I'll be right back. Please don't read it, just throw it in the garbage."

And there's this long silence and Jon says, "It's too late." And my heart just sinks. And he lets me suffer. Then he says, "This is just great." You have to remember, this is New Journalism, it's the '70s. "This is just great. This is just what we're looking for. You've invented a new form. This is fabulous. You've got the job. From now on, I just want you to take this form and stretch it as far as you can."

So, for six years at *New West* magazine, I wrote what must surely have been the strangest restaurant reviews ever written. I wrote stuff from Mars; I wrote stuff that was set in the seventeenth century; I wrote love stories; I wrote westerns. And I had a great time with it.

And then, suddenly, six years later, I had a little following for these reviews. I get a call from the *Los Angeles Times*: Would I like to be their restaurant critic? Now, I have two problems with this: one, I am a Berkeley person and I hate L.A. I mean, if you know anything about California, you know that L.A. and San Francisco have a mutual loathing. And

I have this big San Francisco chip on my shoulder and I'm not about to move down there.

And second, it's a newspaper. I've never really had a real job; I've been freelance my whole life, and the idea of working at a newspaper is a little strange to me. But they finally talked me into it. And I think, *Okay, maybe this will be interesting.*

And I go down. Now, you have to picture this: I have no training as a journalist at all, and I'm about to be the restaurant critic of the largest paper west of the Mississippi, and one of the three or four most important newspapers in the country.

And for my first review, I do exactly what I've always done: I write this little invented story. I was reviewing a restaurant that had been very famous years earlier, and I sort of imagine that Gloria Swanson is with me in the restaurant. And I at least have the sense to show it to a friend who's a reporter before I turn my first opus in to my editors. And my friend, Henry, looks at me and says, "Ruth! This is a newspaper." And I say, "Yeah." And he says, "You can't make stuff up. I mean, you weren't with Gloria Swanson in this restaurant. You can't—that's fine for a magazine, but you can't do it at a newspaper."

So I have to reinvent myself as a critic and learn about journalism. It was a really interesting thing to do, to actually train myself to find what was interesting in the reality to write the review. So I do that and I'm there as the restaurant critic for seven years.

And then Shelby Coffey comes as the editor of the paper, and he blackmails me, essentially, into becoming the food editor of the newspaper. The food section, at that point, was like a little magazine. In those days, there was huge competition among 10 Los Angeles supermarket chains (there's since been a huge consolidation), so each would take out four or five or eight pages of advertising in the newspaper each week. So we had this 60-page food section every week.

And I had a huge staff and a photo studio and a kitchen. And, once again, I have to learn how to do this because I have no idea how to be a food section editor.

When I arrived, it had been a classic women's section, filled with pleasant recipes and helpful hints for things like how to recycle your old nylons into pot scrubbers. And it was very timid. It offended absolutely no one.

The first week I was there, I threw out everything that my predecessor had prepared—I think it was actually on using Coca-Cola in cooking—and sent a reporter out to find out how people on food stamps were eating. And, in the course of the next few months, we completely changed that section into something that was political and really dealt with the community, and was like nothing that that community had ever seen before.

And after the first couple of issues I had one with an old man on the cover, and Shelby came in and he pointed to the word "food" and he pointed to this man, and he said, "This is not this." And I said, "Well, you know, if you think what I'm going to do is fill this section up with pleasant little recipes, find someone else to do it, because I'm not doing that." And he said, "But, Ruth, your readers are just women looking for a little help with their daily cooking." Which was not the right thing to say to me.

So I gave him this speech about how food was a really serious subject. And I said, "I want to cover politics and agriculture and sociology; and I'm not going to be happy until everyone in Los Angeles reads this section. I mean, I don't want this to be a women's section. Men eat too. Everybody eats. Everybody should read this section."

And he backed out of my office, shaking his head. But I had a reporter who was covering the decisions they were making in Washington that affected the price of the food you were buying. And the supermarkets weren't happy about that story. They had thought that they owned this section, and they really didn't want this.

But what happened was that the readers started really liking this section. And after I'd been there about six months, Shelby came in one day and he said—sort of wonderingly, because he's not a person who eats very much—he said he had been to a party the night before where a California Supreme Court judge had told him that it was her favorite section in the paper.

And a few days later, the paper did a focus group where they were trying to get people to talk about how they clipped coupons. And all these women wanted to talk about the actual content of the section. And one woman actually said, "You know, I may never use those Cambodian recipes that you printed last week, but this is really the only section of the newspaper where I find out what the lives of the people all around me are really like."

And the point of this, I think, is that I learned that the only way to do a magazine—because this essentially was a magazine in a newspaper—is not to underestimate your audience, ever (which is one of the things that happens continually in food sections), and to follow your heart. That the only way to have a really good magazine is to print the things you want to read and assume that it will find its own readership.

And I truly believe that food is an important subject. When I came to *The New York Times*, they hired me because Bryan Miller decided he didn't want to do restaurant reviews anymore. They asked me to come, and, once again, I said, "I am not going to review restaurants the way it's been done before in this city. I'm not going to only review high-end restaurants. And I am going to make these reviews very personal. And if that's not what you want, I'm not the person you should hire to do this."

And I came to *The New York Times* and I started writing about Japanese noodle shops and dim sum parlors and little Mexican taco parlors. And writing about them not in the $25 and under category, but as serious reviews and talking about what that food was. I didn't just do it because I loved that food; I made those choices because, to me, they were more important than my own personal taste.

A wide swath of New Yorkers was horrified when I gave three stars for what many readers called a little Japanese noodle joint, which happened to be what I thought of as a fairly perfect restaurant. And I wanted to make a point: when people say that French food is better than Chinese food, they are talking beyond taste. There is meaning hidden underneath each dish.

There is a reason politicians go around munching on pizza and knishes and egg rolls when they are on the campaign trail. We all understand the subtext: with each bite, they are trying to tell us how much they like Italians, Jews, and Chinese people. And there is certainly no better place to start learning about another culture than at the table.

I am not the first to think of this, certainly, but I tell you this because, after I had been the restaurant critic of *The New York Times* for almost seven years, I get a call from James Truman. And I have to tell you that I knew so little about this culture that I had to ask someone who James Truman was. And they said, "Oh, you should probably go talk to him, he's the editorial director of Condé Nast."

So I went to this tea with him and he said, "We have to meet somewhere where no one is going to see us." And I thought, *Hmm, this is really interesting.* So he came right to the point and said, "I'm looking for a new editor for *Gourmet* magazine." And my first reaction was, *Why would I want that? I've got the greatest job on earth: I'm the restaurant critic of* The New York Times. *It's a fabulous job.*

But then I started giving him this lecture, and I said, "You know, I don't want the job, but let me tell you what I think that magazine should be." And I gave him my food-is-political, food-is-sociological, food-is-really-important lines. And I told him what I thought an epicurean magazine for the twenty-first century ought to be. I said, "You can't just have a magazine with a bunch of recipes and pretty pictures." And when I was done with this little speech, James looked at me and said, "Are you sure you don't want this job?"

The thing that actually made me say yes to him was when he said, "I've been looking for a gracious dinner party, but you've convinced me that I ought to be looking for more. Why don't you think about it?"

Then I went back and thought about it. And my deal with *The New York Times* had been that when I got tired of doing restaurant criticism, I would become an editor there. And I thought, *If you're going to be an editor somewhere, wouldn't you rather be an editor at a magazine where you have resources than at a newspaper where*—I knew from my experience at the *Los Angeles Times*—*you're constantly begging people to do things for nothing?*

And I was also interested in it because at that point, I was fifty years old, and I had no idea how to run a magazine. And I thought, *This is going to be an amazing learning curve. And I have no ego involvement in it. If I can't do it, everybody will say, well, they were really stupid, they hired a restaurant critic to be a magazine editor, and of course she couldn't do it.* But I would have a chance to put out the magazine I most wanted to put out, and I would be learning this whole new thing.

But, looking back, I'm really stunned at how much I didn't know. I mean, I didn't even know to ask the kind of questions I should be asking, like: Why are you looking for a new editor?

On the first day I was there, someone mentioned an adjacency. Well, adjacency is probably the most important thing, and I didn't know what it was.

In the magazine, you have the well, which is the part where there are no ads. And then you have the articles that have adjacent ads. And the advertisers fight for these—they want to be adjacent to something that is attractive; they think the people who are reading that article will want to read their ads. There are also all kinds of rules involved. For instance, car manufacturers want seven pages between them and the next car people.

These adjacencies are sold. They are promised, for instance, that they are going to be in the first ten pages, or before the table of contents. And if you wonder why the table of contents is so damned hard to find in any magazine, it is because advertisers pay more to be in front of the table of contents. So one of the things you notice is the tables of contents moving back farther and farther and farther in magazines.

And one of the things that all of us who are magazine editors really admire about Oprah is that she said, "You will put the table of contents on page two." Which all of us would do if we could. But we can't.

Anyway, I didn't know what an adjacency was. And it was only later that I asked, Why are you looking for a new editor? And the reason was that *Gourmet*—which is a magazine that started in 1941 and is sort of the Bible of the epicurean category—had a renewal rate second only to that of *The New Yorker.* I mean, an incredible renewal rate. We have people who've actually been getting the magazine since it started. And the average time of readership is something like eight years, which, in magazine terms, is just incredible.

But the renewals had started going down, just slightly. They did a little research to find out why the renewals were suddenly going down, and what did they discover? People were dying. And they looked at the future and thought: this is not good; we have got to find new, younger readers.

I didn't find out the second reason they hired me until I'd been there about six months and my publisher took me out to Detroit to talk to the car people (who are very, very important for all magazines). And one of the very big honchos in automobile advertising said to me, after he'd had a little bit too much to drink, "If they hadn't brought you into this magazine, you would not have one car ad left in the book." Because the car people were starting to feel that the magazine was tired.

So I realized that what I am supposed to do is change this magazine so that the renewals go back up again. And change it so that the advertisers like the magazine and feel that it's had a new infusion of life and interest, but not change it so much that the 750,000 existing subscribers notice that it's changed. I didn't know it then, but there is nothing more difficult in the entire world than to do this little sleight-of-hand thing, which is to change it but not change it.

In many ways, the fact that I didn't have a magazine background really served me well, because I was too stupid to know how hard it was going to be. And when my publisher took me out to talk to advertisers, I found myself saying, "Well, there's no demographic for food. Food transcends age. It transcends money. It transcends location. There is a food lifestyle, and I'm not going for younger readers and I'm not going for older readers, I'm going to find these people who have understood suddenly in America that food is important."

And the fact that I honestly believe this really helped. But I was just looking around for something I could say to advertisers.

And the next thing I told them is that the only way to run a good magazine is to have a point of view, which I really believe.

And when James hired me, I said, "If you think that you're going to get focus groups to tell me what we should be doing in this magazine, don't look at me. Because the first time you get a focus group in here, I'm out the door. To try to find out what the audience wants and do that magazine—I think that's a really pathetic thing to do. I am going to make the best magazine that I know how to make. And it's going to have to be interesting to me. And if it's not interesting, then you're going to have to find another editor. But I'm not going to start tinkering with the formula."

When James hired me, he said, "You're probably going to have to clean house." By which he meant that I would probably have to come in and fire everybody at the magazine and start fresh.

Well, of course, there were two problems with this: one is I'm not that kind of person—I mean, it's just not what I could imagine myself doing. And, two, of course, I didn't know who I'd hire instead—it was not like I had a big magazine background and fifty people out there to whom I could just say, "Oh, come help me make this magazine."

And I went in to the staff and I called a meeting. Well, the first thing I discovered was they'd never had a meeting before, which struck me as extremely strange. I really believed that one of the great things about magazine work is it's very collaborative. So the idea that they'd never had a meeting just stunned me. And I thought, *Okay, if they've never had a meeting, they're going to expect me to do all the talking.* So I went in with a lot of material, just ready to listen to myself talk for a couple of hours if I had to.

And we sat down in this room and I said, "Okay, we can do anything with this magazine. We have a mandate to make the best magazine. What do you think we should do?" And I didn't open my mouth again for three hours, at which point I said, "This meeting has gone on too long."

What I had was a staff with this pent-up energy. They were dying to make a good magazine, and they had hundreds and hundreds of ideas. And basically, what we did was do the articles that they essentially told me to do.

One of the great things about Condé Nast is that they let everybody run their magazine the way they want to run the magazine. And I read these articles about Anna Wintour and Graydon Carter, and they run completely different operations.

I am a big believer in hiring good people and listening to them and empowering them. We take an idea, we shape it together. The art director brings something. And it's also very important, I think, for people to be able to say, "That is the dopiest idea you've ever had." And my staff says that to me all the time.

My first job at *Gourmet* was to modernize it. I was stunned when I got there: they didn't use computers, they did everything on paper. They had computers but they weren't using them. And if you were an editor and you wanted to make a change, you had to go to the production people and they input the changes.

So we changed that. We started using computers. This magazine did not have a photo editor, which is sort of stunning at a magazine that is so dependent on photography. It didn't have a fact checker, which was amazing. It didn't have any copyeditors—the editors would sort of copy-edit and fact check. So I completely reorganized the magazine in that sense, and we now have a photo department and a copy department and a fact department, which allows the editors to be editors and spend time finding writers and talking to writers and thinking about what we should have in the magazine.

And part of my sense of what I'm supposed to do is make it a really fun place to work. I think we're dealing with something that's fun to talk about and to read about. And I think you get a real sense from a magazine if the staff is having a good time doing it. So we started spending a lot of money that had been spent in other ways to get the staff traveling.

For instance, when we do a Rome issue, everybody on the staff goes to Rome. We have ten full-time cooks, and they went to Rome and they rented an apartment with a kitchen and went out and tasted the food and went shopping and figured out how to make recipes. And the travel editor goes out and sleeps in all these hotels. And, in fact, one of the drags of the Rome issue is that while everybody gets to go to Rome, you have to change hotels every night. Because if we're writing about hotels, we want to try the hotels. And so it sounds really glamorous that you're going to Rome, but changing hotels can take you about half the day. So it has a downside.

But what is my major job at the magazine? A lot of my job is selling the magazine. A lot of my job is being a partner to the publisher. And I spend a lot of time going to Detroit and glamorous places like Torrance, where there are a lot of car advertising people, and telling them how great the magazine is and why they should be buying ads in it.

And it turns out that the biggest asset I brought to the magazine was not my background as a newspaper journalist or as a food editor or as a freelance magazine writer. The biggest asset I brought to the magazine was actually my background as an author. And there are two reasons for this. One is that the books had a really wide circulation, and because they were so personal, it made people feel like they knew me, which is very good when you go out to talk to advertisers.

But more than that, when you're an author, you go on book tours. You go to six or seven or eight cities and you do ten appearances a day where you talk to people and, essentially, beg them to buy your book. And when you're a magazine editor, you spend a lot of time going to cities and doing eight or ten or fifteen visits a day to groups of different kinds of advertising people, begging them to buy your magazine. And it's remarkably similar. I would say the most important thing I brought to it was this experience of being on book tours.

The reaction of *Gourmet*'s readership to the changes in the magazine—well, a magazine like *Gourmet* has a very devoted readership. In the first few months I was there, the mail was voluminous. We would get perhaps fifty letters a day; some of them six pages, single-spaced, telling me exactly what people liked and didn't like about the changes. And if you start listening to that, you go crazy. All you can do is do the best that you can.

At one point, I actually said to my secretary, "The next letter that comes that says, 'if it ain't broke, don't fix it,' I don't want to see," because I heard that so many times in the first year I was there. Because although I thought that the magazine needed a new voice, there were hundreds of thousands of people who loved it exactly the way it was. And if I'd listened to them, I never would have changed it.

Apart from *Gourmet*, I'm writing a book these days about my disguises as a restaurant critic [*Garlic and Sapphires: The Secret Life of a Critic in Disguise*, published in 2005]. When I was on my way to become the restaurant critic of *The New York Times*, I was sitting on the plane to New York and this woman sitting next to me said, "I know who you are, and I know where you're going." And I said, "What are you talking about?"

And she said, "I'm a waitress at a restaurant in New York, and we have your picture hanging in the kitchen. And we all know that you're coming to New York to review restaurants, and we're all watching for you, and if you think that one of those big hats is going to protect you, forget it. This is not Los Angeles, and we're watching for you."

And I got really irritated, and I got off the plane and called one of my mother's best friends, who's an acting coach, and I said, "I need to look like someone else." And she said, "Oh, I'll be right over." And she told me where to buy wigs and she brought me a makeup person who showed me how to turn myself into someone else.

And I did—I think my fifth review in New York was of Le Cirque. It had four stars, it had always been, everybody loved it, every critic loved it. So I go in there as the first of my disguises, a Midwestern housewife called Molly. And Molly went in with a woman friend, and we were nobody. And they treated us like dirt. They made us wait forty-five minutes for a table and then they gave us this little tiny table in the back of the room.

And the thing that really, really got Molly angry was that she got a wine list, and the wine list at Le Cirque takes you about twenty minutes just to read through once. And I had it about a minute and the maitre d' came up and took it out of my hands and said, "I need that," and took it to some men four tables away. And I kept saying, "Excuse me? Excuse me?" And I was not me, I was Molly. If it were me, I would have just gone up and snatched it back and said, "Excuse me, that's my wine list." But Molly was very well behaved and she kept sort of timidly saying, "Excuse me, excuse me, could I—." Half an hour later, she gets the wine list.

And so I went many times as Molly, and never had a good experience. The food was fine, but I don't believe people go out to eat; they go out for an experience.

For my last visit, I decided that I would not make the reservation in my name but I would go as myself. And I knew that they had the picture of me hanging in the kitchen. So I got my 30-year-old nephew to make a reservation, and he said, "I could only get a 9:45 reservation." And I said, "Well, that's fine." And he said, "Let's go early and just see what happens."

So we go early and there are a hundred people milling around, waiting to be seated at the restaurant. And Sirio, the owner, spots me through the crowd. And he parts the crowd and comes through and takes my hand and leads me forward and says, "The King of Spain is waiting in the bar, but your table is ready," and seats us at a four-top. Everywhere I've been seated before has been miserable little twos in the back of the room. But now, just the two of us, we're at a four-top. And I say to Johnnie, my nephew, "The King of Spain is waiting in the bar, sure." And Johnnie turns around and he says, "That *is* the King of Spain. I saw him on TV last night." And we have this splendid, splendid experience. They're dancing around us, they're sending us little extra tidbits, could they send us some wine.

So I write parallel reviews. One, what happened when Molly went, and she writes the review. And one, what happened to the restaurant critic of *The New York Times*. The uproar was unbelievable. As it turns out— and I didn't know this at the time, or I probably would have had some hesitation in doing this—but Le Cirque is a favorite restaurant of Punch Sulzberger. And my editors were terrified. I mean, they had not really vetted any of my things; they vetted this one. And they were making little changes. I mean, I know that this was read. Max Frankel read this one. They were terrified.

And consequently, I did not sleep for two nights. I thought, *Why have I done this?* I knew if I'd made one tiny mistake, my career was over. I mean, I had just come to New York, nobody knew who I was. I was truly terrified. The next day I couldn't even call my machine to find out what the response to this had been. I was in such a bad place.

Finally, about three o'clock, I call my machine to see. And the tape had run out, there were so many phone messages on it. But the first one was from Warren Hoge, who was the assistant managing editor who had hired me. And he said, "The first phone call that the publisher got this morning was from Walter Annenberg, who said, 'That is the best review this newspaper has ever published.'" Apparently, they had not recognized him at some point and treated him like dirt. So Warren said, "No matter what happens now, it's fine."

Ruth Reichl returned six years later to give another lecture to the Delacorte students. In it, she made clear how things had changed.

I thought it would help if I told you what I did today. I got up in the morning, and I Twittered. Why did I Twitter? I Twittered because my publisher thinks that this is very good for the magazine, that by Twittering I can send people to Gourmet.com, that it will increase our traffic. So I got up this morning and I Twittered.

And then I walked to work, because it's basically the only exercise I get all day. I walked into my office, which is certainly the most deluxe office I've ever had, and is right on the corner of Forty-second Street and Broadway—there are so many neon signs surrounding me that I can work in there at night without turning on the lights.

And there were all kinds of proofs from the May issue of *Gourmet* sitting on my desk, so I read these and made notes on them. While I was doing that, I got a call from the head of human resources, telling me the very sad news that Condé Nast was canceling its tuition reimbursement program for employees. So I had to announce this to my staff. And it's sad for everyone, but especially for the cooks—we have twelve full-time people down in the kitchen—and they have used this to go and take cooking lessons all over the world.

I had a meeting about the new cocktail thing that we're about to put up on the Web. We started Gourmet.com a little over a year ago, and we're constantly trying to figure out ways to get more traffic to it. And at Christmas this year, we put up a thing about cookies, where we chose the best cookie from every year of the magazine's history. And it's driven a lot of traffic, so we decided to do the same thing for cocktails. So I had to have a meeting about that.

Then we had a meeting about the Cookbook Club, which is another way that we are trying to create a community, because one of the things you really want to do these days with magazines is create a sense of community with your readers. So we started this Cookbook Club where we test cookbooks and choose a cookbook a month. And we've also created a giveaway, where if you go online and register, we give away a cookbook a day with the cookbook of the month.

The thing about this that is amazing is that we test these cookbooks and about 90 percent of them don't work. I have made a pact with everybody on staff that we choose a couple of cookbooks every month and anybody who cooks from them, we'll pay for the ingredients. So we have, at any given time, thirty or forty different people cooking the recipes from the book. It is stunning how few books work. Well, the cookbook we tested this week was a complete disaster. A beautiful book, but not one recipe worked. So now we can't find a book for August—a big disaster, what are we going to do?

Then somebody came running into my office very excitedly to say that there was a peregrine falcon on the ledge across Forty-second Street, eating a pigeon, and that I had to come look at this. And it was amazing, we were all gathered there looking at this bird. Feathers were flying. Then I got a call from my coproducer at WGBH. We are just finishing our third season of Gourmet's *Diary of a Foodie*, and we edited this. We had a two-hour phone call where we edited. They send us the rough cut and we edit it and give them notes. It's a very long procedure.

Then I went down into the test kitchen and had a discussion with Paul, one of our cooks who is currently doing Christmas cookies for next year. He's been making these chestnut cookies, and he didn't think they were crisp enough. So we had a big discussion about what he could do to make them crisper. Then I came back and Twittered about that. Then I wrote yet another letter of apology to a reader about the Korean layout. If you look at this issue, we have made what turns out to be a truly bad mistake.

The woman who did this Korean food is a Chinese woman, but she lived in Korea for about ten years and cooked in restaurants in Korea. But the art department did not hire Korean models when they did it, and the Korean community is very upset about that. And we usually do very good research, but they got so carried away with the beauty of this. And they also used a lot of red, and Koreans consider red the color of death. So I've been getting a lot of letters from people online. And I've been answering them all.

And the thing that's stunning about it is, people are so surprised to get a letter back from the editor-in-chief that they always write me back very thoughtful letters. And what's odd, one of our cooks in the test kitchen is Korean American, and of course we should have had her look at the layout. But we didn't. And we deliberately didn't assign her this, because you don't want to have this situation where you're having only Chinese cooks cooking Chinese food and only Korean cooks cooking Korean food and French ones doing French. I mean, that's sort of silly. But we should have had Kay look at it, and it was just a mistake.

I had a meeting about *Appetite for Living*, which is another TV show we're about to start shooting. This is one where I'm going to go around the world cooking in various cooking schools. But we have sold it to American Airlines with celebrities attached, and we have to find the celebrities who will come. This was a big mistake too.

Then the make-up lady came, because my publisher, who likes to drag me around the country with her selling ads, realized that since I have to go around the world now cooking in cooking schools, I can't come with her. So she hired a TV crew to film me talking about the magazine, so she can have a virtual me when she goes out to sell ads.

And then I started writing cookie copy for the cookie book, because we just sold this online cookie project we did as a book. But it has to be done in a week, and all the headnotes need to be rewritten. So I started working on that. Then I fielded three phone calls from the editor of *Gourmet Today*, which is a big cookbook coming out in September, with more than twelve hundred recipes. And she didn't like the introduction I wrote, so we had a discussion about that.

Then I had a meeting with my publisher to discuss budget cuts. Budget cuts are a new and horrible reality at Condé Nast. She just had a meeting with the CFO, who asked her to cut a million dollars out of her budget. And I can't cut a million dollars out of mine, but we started talking about where I could take the money out. Then I went back down to the kitchen and tasted the squid soup that's going into an article about a cooking school in Tuscany in May. And I Twittered about that.

Then my managing editor came and said, "We've got four pages too many in the May issue. What are you going to take out?" The ads are even lower than the very bad estimate. So it's horrible. You sit there saying, "We can't do an issue without this and this and this." But you have to take pages out. Came back, wrote more cookie copy. Twittered again. Had a meeting with the art director about what we're going to put on the cover for June. Walking down the hall, I ran into one of the people we just laid off, whose last day is tomorrow. And it's terrible; she's wonderful, we all feel awful about it. And it was just this very horrible discussion.

By then I tried writing more cookie copy. I was trying to get through all the heads for the sixties today, but I only got to sixty-four. And I just realized I was too tired to do it, and nothing was coming. And then I tried to figure out what I was going to say to you tonight, and I wrote this list.

So I've told you this, to tell you that when I spoke to this group six years ago, the list of what I did today would have been utterly and completely different. In those days, I was editing a magazine, and everything I had to do was about editing the magazine. And today, almost nothing that I do has to do with editing a magazine. My role is now pretty much long-term planning, thinking about the issues, dealing with the art director. But it is no longer about my sitting there and writing every caption. I do read every final, but that will often be the first time I've seen the captions. And six years ago, there was nothing that I didn't see and agonize over. So it's very much a changing role.

And in the video that my publisher is going to take out on the road, the director asked me, "Where will the magazine be ten years from now?" And all I could say is, "I don't have a clue."

3

How to Become the Editor-in-Chief of Your Favorite Women's Magazine

Roberta Myers is the editor-in-chief/VP of Brand Content of *Elle* magazine. She began her career as an editorial assistant at *Rolling Stone* and was an editor at *Interview*, the managing editor of *Seventeen*, and a senior editor at *InStyle* magazine. Before joining *Elle* in 2000, she was the editor-in-chief of *Mirabella* magazine. Roberta Myers delivered her talk on April 26, 2007.

How many of you read fashion magazines? And how many of you think that fashion magazines are basically bad for women? I want to talk about that. And a bit about my career, with the hope that my crooked path to editor-in-chief may somewhat illuminate the magazine business. And about *Elle*, with the hope that it might shed some light on the kind of work you can find in fashion and women's magazines. And then I'm going to tell you how to flatter an editor to get a job.

I went to college at a big land-grant school in the West, on a diving scholarship. I didn't go to graduate school, as you all are. I came to New York armed with my political science degree, membership in the National Political Science Honor Society, and a strong desire to work in magazines: *The Nation* or *The New Republic* or *Time*.

I had a cousin who was a writer for *Self*, and her life seemed as glamorous and fun as that of anyone I knew personally, and she promised me that if I moved to New York, it would be no problem for her to get me an entry-level job at Condé Nast. The legendary HR department there, she explained, really liked to hire family, as they had done with her. Her stepmother, Edith Lowe Gross Myers, was a longtime writer at *Vogue*, who, tragically, had a heart attack in the *Vogue* bathroom, hit her head on the sink, and died.

My mother was one of those second-wave feminists who told their daughters to not learn how to type, lest they end up in the secretarial pool their whole lives. But I flunked the typing test, and all the tests I guess, so now I really had to get a job. I maniacally read the "Help Wanted" ads and worked at Lord & Taylor in "better dresses" until I finally got an offer to work in the advertising department at *McCall's*, a job I accepted but never actually started. I'd had my heart set on editorial. My cousin knew somebody at *Rolling Stone* named Jann, and gave me his direct number. I spent a good five minutes scanning the masthead for a person whose name began with Y, until I realized it was the guy at the top. I called his office; it was 7:30 at night, and for some bizarre reason, he picked up his own phone. I explained who I was and why I was calling. He said, barked, to send my resume, and slammed down the phone.

I'm sure he didn't expect me to show up the next day in my little black dress with a little bow on the back, holding my resume. I told Jann's assistant that I had an appointment. She looked at me sort of confused, but let me come in to talk to her. An assistant had just quit, she said, but she was too busy to give me a typing test. Could I come back on Monday?

I went to Barnes & Noble and bought a used teach-yourself-to-type book for $1.97. I spent the weekend in the apartment my cousin shared with her boyfriend—Q-W-E-R-T-Y—teaching myself to type. They hired me, for around $8,000 a year, which even then was a terrible salary, but it was an amazing two-and-a-half-year beginning to my career.

I worked first for the music editor, Jim Henke, who now runs the Rock and Roll Hall of Fame, and then for the insanely talented features editor, Carolyn White, who was married to the Pulitzer Prize–winning writer Richard Ben Cramer. I couldn't decide which one of them I wanted to be.

Along with opening mail, fetching coffee, and, well, typing, it was my job to transcribe writers' interviews. I got to hear this new singer, Bono, talk into the night. Hunter Thompson's famed mojo machine—really an earsplitting Stone Age fax—was outside my boss's office, and I was humbled to be the person Hunter would call to say that something was coming. The magazine's values were what I thought every editor's were: that institutions were to be challenged; that popular culture deserved serious and detailed examination; that the only rich and powerful people who weren't suspect were rock stars; and that rock 'n' roll was a true engine for social change.

Rolling Stone had just moved to Manhattan from San Francisco, bringing along some of the most important journalists and photographers in magazines, including Hunter and Annie Leibovitz. There were a few stoners in ripped T-shirts left over from California, but they mostly, it seemed, worked in the art department. I identified with them and dressed like them, but the place was really run by young, pretty Ivy League guys in buttoned-down shirts. At a magazine that fought for social justice, there were only a handful of women who held a title higher than editorial assistant, and there were no people of color.

Even though I was an assistant, the work was never boring. I got to report small news items, meet rock stars, hang around MTV, and go to three legendary Christmas parties. But after three incredibly fun, educational years, I left to go to *Interview*. They gave me a little going-away party at which I cried, but Carolyn White said to me, "Why the hell are you crying? You're going to get into even better parties now!" The salary was still lousy, but I was going to be a real editor, and the only phone I was going to have to answer was my own.

I arrived, of course, full of righteous editorial steam, ready to assign and edit the kinds of stories I'd just been retyping and fact-checking at *Rolling Stone*, only to discover that not only was there little journalism in the magazine, there was barely any writing at all. I worked at *Interview* when Andy Warhol was still alive, and very much a presence in the magazine. *Interview* was in the same building as the Factory, where they were cranking out his multimillion-dollar portraits of socialites and rock stars, and where the glamorous and the famous mingled with rising artists

(I spent several evenings in Jean-Michel Basquiat's apartment), up-and-coming novelists (Jay McInerney), and underpaid flunkies like me.

One of the first stories I worked on was an interview with someone very high up in the Reagan administration—because I was "political." The story discussed nothing more political than good tables in Washington, popular office decorations, and vacation sites. When I had a small fit —but . . . but . . . Star Wars! The Iran Contra Affair! The Truth!—the art director and the funniest person on the planet, Marc Balet, clapped his big hand on my shoulder and said, "That's so depressing; people don't want to think about that stuff all the time."

And so I was introduced to the world of style magazines. When I got over my superiority complex, I found myself in the world of image and images, which was as complex and rich and nuanced as writing. Only in retrospect did I realize that it was, in fact, in an exclusive, influential club that defined a genuine cultural moment in New York.

In my first month, I was sent to assist famed photographer Robert Mapplethorpe on a photo shoot. He moved quietly and deliberately, and we set up almost in silence. He was shooting Patti Hansen, who had just had a baby. She came into the studio, and with her red hair and freckles she looked sort of like my mother. She was beautiful, but sort of normal compared to what I'd expected. The hair and makeup people got to work on her, and in two hours she was transformed into a goddess.

A few months later I was sent to style a fashion story—based on heroes of the American Revolution, to be played by up-and-coming actors such as Stephen Dorff—at the last minute. I was pulling racks of clothing from a costume shop with my co-worker, who, as we went through the looks, regaled me with stories of his late-night job as a go-go dancer. But neither of us really knew exactly what else the stylist was to do. So much so that the mother of Lisa Bonet yelled at us because we were shooting her daughter without a hairstylist or makeup artist. I told her it was part of the story—women didn't wear makeup during the Revolution.

At *Interview* I learned the differences between the two kinds of people who go into magazine editorial, the words people and the visual people, and woe be to the editor who doesn't understand the primal attachment those in both camps have to the superiority of their point of view. It's usually the words people who end up being editor-in-chief, which is interesting because at the big national glossies, most of the budget is spent on photography.

Perhaps the biggest problem with new editor-in-chiefs have is that until they become the boss, they have little actual experience with the overall visual direction of the magazine. But magazines are as much a visual product as a written one, and the magazines that will survive the Internet are going to be those that understand the primacy of the image.

Interview was populated mostly by gorgeous gay men and slightly damaged young women. I shared a tiny office with one of the former, and we became as familiar as siblings, squabbling and sharing food in equal measure. One day, I went to take a bite of his hamburger, and he said to me, "I wouldn't do that." I said, "Why not?" He said, "Well, there's this thing going around, this gay cancer, and we don't really know how you get it, so maybe we should stop sharing our lunch." Within in a year, men we all knew were infected with HIV. Within five, the artistic and creative life of downtown New York was decimated.

I worked at *Interview* for almost three years. It was fun and fascinating, but also really difficult and personality driven. One day I got a phone call from a recruiter about a job at a magazine for teenagers. It was an editor-in-chief's job at a recent start-up, a job my office mate said I wouldn't get. It was a magazine called *Careers*, which was owned by the heir to the Stetson hat fortune. He wanted to do something good for teenagers, a little magazine about different careers one could pursue after high school and college.

Can you think of anything less cool than a magazine aimed at teenagers about what kind of job options they might have, postcollege? But I was going to be the editor. All mine, at twenty-six. I faced social death, for sure—no more VIP access to Area!—but I learned how to put together a whole magazine, from my first cover shoot with two models, a boy and a girl (the boss said it was too sexy, but we still ran it) to what I thought was a pretty thorough guide to things to do with your life. I was there about nine months before joining *Seventeen* to be first a features editor, then head of the department. I stayed there for six years and was eventually promoted to managing editor.

It was an unruly group of talented, smart young women and one man. It was my first experience running a big staff, trying to corral the work and ambitions of fashion, beauty, and features editors who were deeply competitive with one another for magazine real estate and recognition. If you have any notion that journalism is a calling or that you want to do this kind of work to help people, there's no better audience than teenagers. For many girls, *Seventeen* was the first magazine that was theirs, a magazine they bought and read on their own, that talked about the wider world as they might actually live it. One of every two teenage girls in America read *Seventeen*. Future Supreme Court justices and future astronauts and future senators and future homemakers and future Republicans—they all read it.

And much to the dismay of readers' parents, the magazine talked frankly about sex, drugs, relationships, violence, and peer pressure, along with all those cute shoes. The reader is passionate, responsive, and utterly devoted, and *Seventeen* reaches and impacts her at a time when she's still forming her worldview. At *Seventeen* I learned that I could cover almost any story in the news—national, international, elections, anything I wanted—as long as I could isolate what it was in the story that would be relevant and tell it in a way that would be compelling for the readers.

And we always knew what was compelling to the readers because they wrote to us. *Seventeen* had two editors whose full-time job was to answer reader mail. We got so much of it—literally thousands of letters— and most of it was pretty repetitive: How do I get a boy to like me? How do I get a boy I don't like to stop liking me? How do I get that cute haircut that Hillary Duff has?, et cetera. As a person who thinks of herself as feminist, I spent the first two years I was there trying to reframe the questions. "Who cares how you get a boy to like you? Do you like him?"

But some of the letters were quite serious. Young women who were being sexually abused by their fathers and didn't know what to do; girls who were pregnant and didn't know what to do; girls who were drug addicts and didn't know what to do. The magazine was genuinely a resource, and an incredible responsibility, if you think about it. We had a guy put in jail for raping his daughter. She reached out to us, and we reached out to the social service agencies that could help her.

And at *Seventeen*, I also realized that those beauty credits on the photographs—"Jessica Simpson is wearing Super-Smoky Eyeliner"—were made up. This was devastating to me. We don't tell the truth?! I'd been one of those girls who tore out the page and took it to the makeup counter looking for the Super-Smoky Eyeliner in retro black so I could put it on exactly the right way. There was a lot to learn.

I left *Seventeen* to do a start-up with Hachette, the company that owns *Elle*. We did the first ever (I was told) joint venture between a television network, NBC, and a publishing company. We named it *Tell*, and it was run through Hachette's custom publishing division. NBC was promoting their teenage programming, things like *Blossom* and *Saved by the Bell*. It was a one-year deal. Most editors are terrified by the words "custom publishing." It connotes advertiser control of the edit, which can be true, but since our partner was a big news organization they never even asked to see a lineup. They did, however, make a request: Could we please put one of their young stars on our first cover? For me, this was great—Will Smith had a hit show, *The Fresh Prince of Bel-Air*; he had a hit song, "Parents Just Don't Understand"; and he was releasing a little movie called *Independence Day*. He was a real star, an actual star, and NBC would give him to me—unheard of for a magazine that didn't even exist yet.

We shot it, wrote it, mocked up the cover, and then I went to show it to the publisher as a courtesy. She said nothing, and left the room.

Minutes later I was called to a meeting "upstairs." I'd never been "upstairs." There was basically a conference room filled with suits, men from marketing and circulation and some other important-sounding divisions whom I'd never met. They asked me about the cover. I said, "Will Smith! He has a movie coming out, he's on this hit television show, he's a huge star! We never could have gotten him, a little magazine like this, blah-blah-blah. . . ." Somebody said, "Well, he's black. Black people don't sell magazines."

I started to have one of those experiences where the room begins to spin; my heart was racing and my stomach started to hurt. I literally didn't know what to do. I was really still pretty inexperienced. I was thinking, *Oh my god, I have to quit my job. I'll never get to be the editor of a magazine ever again. My career is over. But I have to leave.* I did the professional thing:

burst into tears and left the meeting. I went back to my office and just sat there, hot-faced with shame that I worked in an industry where things like this were actually said. Then my phone rang. It was the voice of god, i.e., Jean-Louis Ginibre, the longtime editorial director of Hachette. He hadn't been in the meeting, but apparently he'd heard about it, and he said in his thick French accent, "Robbie, I will support you no matter what, as long as you do what is right for your readers."

So Will Smith remained on the cover. It sold. The project lasted a year; we did four issues and then it was over. But what Jean-Louis said to me was another important thing I've learned again and again in my career: you can't edit a magazine to impress people; you can't edit a magazine to show your friends how clever you are or what access you were able to get. You really do have to edit to, and for, your reader.

When the contract was up, I had no job. I went to see Adam Moss. He wasn't a friend of mine. At that time, he was the editor of *The New York Times Magazine*, and he was nice enough to see me every couple of years, when I'd go and try to convince him to give me a job to get me out of the women's magazine ghetto.

He never hired me, but this time he said, "You know, I have a lot of good friends who've had amazing careers at women's magazines, and they do really good work. You shouldn't be such a snob." It wasn't an epiphany, but as I started to move up at women's books, his words stayed with me. Women are important, and it's important to do good magazines for women. I'm always amazed when people seem surprised that *Elle* is "smart." How depressing, that so many people, including women, have such low expectations—for women.

I interviewed at the Time, Inc. start-up *InStyle*, and was hired as a senior editor in fashion. What that meant was pretty wide open; the magazine wasn't doing traditional sittings with models and stylists at the time—everything had a celebrity bent. Time, Inc., as you know, is the storied Temple of Journalism on Sixth Avenue, founded by Henry Luce. The place was filled with legendary reporters and art directors who'd seemingly never seen a fashion editor before. Certainly not in the building. And suddenly all these young women in short skirts and high heels were clicking all around the offices. The men just seemed bemused, but many of the women seemed furious. I was fascinated by the Time, Inc. culture, and the fact that *InStyle* demanded the same reporting and fact-checking rigor of *Time* and *Fortune*, and when I was on the phone with Cybill Shepherd getting the number of pairs of shoes she had, damn it, she'd better be on her knees in the closet counting them. And sending the Polaroids as backup.

InStyle, of course, turned out to be one of the most successful magazine launches in the last fifteen years, and it remade the fashion magazine category. Fashion is an insular, closed society of style and aesthetics—but "taste" is a highly subjective idea. *InStyle* democratized fashion, stripping away some of the mystery while making it accessible to a mass audience. It was there that I also saw the necessity—and power—of marketing. Dollar for dollar, they spent as much marketing the magazine as they did making it. I couldn't get a decent seat at a fashion show, but we got great seats at the Elton John Foundation Oscar fundraiser, because the magazine sponsored it, at $30,000 a table. Through advertising (I'd never worked at a magazine that advertised itself), promotion, events, and, most importantly, the product, the profile of *InStyle* seemed to rise almost overnight. And readers loved it. All of the editors are front-row now. At *InStyle*, I learned how to take a punch from a celebrity publicist. No celebrity does anything for a magazine just because they feel like it; they always have a project to promote, a piece of their image they want to shine or change, which is why all the former teen actresses from NBC's teen programming end up half naked on *Maxim*. I learned who all the important publicists were and who they represented, which turned out to be an unbelievably valuable thing. I watched as *InStyle* threw what seemed like a party a week with various celebrities and various causes, and I watched a PR department in very high gear. And I watched an editor, Martha Nelson, never waver from the mission of that magazine; she knew exactly what it needed to be.

When I left *InStyle*, it was for my first job at *Elle*. I joined as a senior editor, assigning and editing features, from fashion to politics to art, and a front-of-book culture section called "First." My husband, who was at the time still my boyfriend, says that of all my jobs, this was the one at which I seemed to have the most fun. I had my own little fiefdom, and was assigning and editing stories that had something to do with my own life, writers I'd long admired— Susan Minot, Toni Morrison, Jane Smiley. It turned out that Pulitzer Prize winners loved to write for *Elle*, and they too valued a female audience. I was high enough on the masthead to have some autonomy about who and what I covered, and low enough to be insulated from the power struggles and the budget problems and the management issues above me.

Imagine my surprise when one Friday afternoon I was called into my boss's office, told to shut the door, and then told that I would be named the editor of *Mirabella* on Monday. My first reaction was, "I don't want to do this." I'd originally been hired at *Elle* by the editor who was now the editor of *Mirabella*, the first boss I'd ever worked for who I was close enough to and worked closely enough with that I felt was really a mentor to me. She said, "Trust me, you do want this, and your turning it down won't change a thing." I honestly didn't even know that my former boss was considering leaving *Mirabella* or that upper management had even paid attention to who I was.

There was something of a cult around *Mirabella* because it was a magazine that was edited for "older" women—ahem, over thirty. It was home for probably every great essayist and female journalist, and we never lost readers in the almost four years that I was there. But the fashion and beauty advertisers were very vocal about our being "too old," and we bowed to their pressure to go younger—an editor's first mistake. Advertisers are usually called "the client," but as my then CEO, Jack Kliger, said to me: "The reader is our client. We just rent them out to the advertisers." His point, once again, is that you must edit for your audience.

The core of that magazine was really a woman who was 35-plus who had a lot of money. She was sophisticated. She was a consumer of the arts and she had $2,000 to spend on a handbag if she felt like it. Unfortunately, the magazine folded. But they didn't blame me, I guess, because when they folded the magazine, they let me take over *Elle*.

I've been at *Elle* for seven years. And what is *Elle*? It's a core fashion book. Fashion is our promise, and our readers are passionate about it. The only metaphor I can give you is that we cover it the same way that sportswriters cover sports. There are a lot of people, probably in this room, who'd say "fashion journalism" is an oxymoron, but I'll tell you, in the same way that a sportswriter will argue and argue that A-Rod made the second out in the third inning of the third game of the American League playoffs against the Tampa Bay Rays, not the third out in the second inning, fashion editors will fight to the death that it was Oscar de la Renta who did the empire waist six seasons ago, not Carolina Herrera. There's a deep body of knowledge there.

My very first cover for *Elle*, in October 2000, was a photograph of Britney Spears in a Givenchy couture dress. Say what you will about Britney, and the fashion world had a lot to say about it, but we got everyone's attention. And it was meant to be provocative. Not for its own sake, but because to me, fashion is nothing if not an ongoing provocation and conversation about where women are in the culture at this very minute. Britney in couture was a collision of two seemingly opposed poles of popular culture—high fashion and pop music—and it made a statement about how *Elle* was going to proceed with our part of the discussion. Fashion, by definition, is "that which is current," which is really the through line of our magazine. The runway and the street, the juxtaposition of high art and pop culture—I was charged with bringing a fresh point of view to a formula that had gotten a little too predictable. We hired a new creative director and a new design director just this year and are hard at work on a redesign, even though we've had a good couple of years at *Elle*. Another thing I learned from my CEO: the time to change is not when you're doing badly, but when you're doing well, as it's a moment to take risks. We've had 15 quarters of uninterrupted growth on the newsstand, and double-digit advertising growth too. The other magazines in our core set are *Vogue, Harper's Bazaar,* and *W. Vogue* and *Harper's Bazaar* are both over 100 years old. *Vogue* is called the "fashion Bible," and the power and influence of its editor cannot be overstated. But we're a tough competitor. And despite the image of *The Devil Wears Prada,* the movie is not *my* life.

Harper's Bazaar is for an older woman. *W* has an edgier take on fashion. And *Elle* is known as having the youngest point of view, and we are all about helping women build their personal style, not adopting any house style. I'm happy we've also been called "the smart one." In our expanded competitive set are *InStyle, Marie Claire,* and *Glamour.*

Elle was started forty-five years ago by a Frenchwoman named Helene Lazareff, who said she wanted to "open women's appetites." In France, the magazine is a weekly. There are now thirty-eight editions around the world, but *Elle* U.S. is number one in terms of circulation and advertising revenue. We also export the most images—our shoots are in *Elle*s all around the world.

I actually want to talk for a minute about those fake makeup credits, about whether—or when—I sold my soul to the devil.

When I went to my first shoot with Robert Mapplethorpe and saw how a woman was made up for a photograph, I realized it would be impossible to credit all of the products that they use. Unless a makeup artist works with just one particular brand (as many do), you couldn't even identify all of the products, because makeup artists bring a suitcase full of stuff, lay it all out, and then mix them all up to get the right colors and tones for each photograph. The beauty department works with the art department to get the closest approximation of a particular color or look, and then recommends products to match it. And even if we know all the products come from one brand, the lighting or the model's skin tone may change the color so much from what's in the tube as to be unrecognizable. But we do write those credits.

Can I work for a fashion magazine and still call myself a feminist?

At *Seventeen*, readers kept asking us questions like, How do I get a boy to like me? And I kept saying, "Stop asking that question, that's not important. Do you like yourself? Do you know who you want to be?" But they never stopped asking. They always cared. And grownup women—professional, accomplished women—ask the same things. They care, and while I wanted to, as an editor, try to change the conversation and talk people out of their feelings, I slowly realized that I was wrong. Men like to look at women, and a lot of women enjoy it. That's one of the reasons they like to get dressed up and wear makeup. They're not weak or superficial if they want to be attractive. You can have a meaningful career, a complex interior life, and a hot body. Today, everyone talks about the brand. I didn't know I was the brand manager until I went to a conference in France probably a decade ago where they were talking about the success of *Elle*, and they put up on the screen the "brand wheel."

In the middle of the wheel was the word *Elle*, and the spokes of the wheel were the magazine and the show *Project Runway* and the Web site, *Elle*.com. And one was a cell phone. Today the editor-in-chief of a big, successful, broad magazine like ours—1.1 million circulation, 6 million readers—is expected to oversee all of these "extensions." Somebody told me that if I needed resources and money for *Elle*, all I had to do was go to the 45th floor (where the CEO sits) and yell "digital," and they'd throw a pile of money at me.

Magazine companies are scrambling. They're scared. Some of them are losing readers, some of them are losing advertisers. But if you look at what's happening in the fashion magazine category the last few years, the whole category is up. I'd like to say we're up more than the rest of them. I'm going to have to say that because we're having a good couple of years, but we haven't always, and again, I folded a magazine. So I know what it's really like.

I just interviewed sixteen people to be my assistant because my assistant left to go start a Web site for Gawker to cover women's magazines and media. She spent a year basically as the person closest to me—she knows my dress size, who my doctors are. It's a little terrifying, but I'm presuming she'll do the right thing. I interviewed so many people because I can—so many people apply, I have a very strong candidate pool, which is surprising because the actual work is pretty straightforward assistant stuff. And because so many candidates are the friends of industry VIPs—could I please see so-and-so's son, etc.—I must see them.

I was shocked at how bad people were in these interviews. They'd come from very good schools, with maybe six or seven internships behind them. But I wasn't surprised that many of them didn't have a job yet. So here are the few things I'd like to say if you're going to come interview with me.

Please lie to me and tell me you've read the magazine at least once before preparing for the interview. When I ask you, "Why does a smart, Ivy-educated person like yourself want to answer my phone and fetch my coffee for the next years?" don't say, "It's a means to an end." You're *my* means to an end.

When I ask you, "Is there anything you'd like to ask me?" don't say, "When do I get to write?" "How long before I can get promoted?" or, the worst, "No." Say, "I loved your story on Joan Didion's new memoir. Why is that right for your audience?" Or, "I Googled you and read that the May issue was up 15 percent and your competition was down 9 percent, what does that mean?"

Be persistent. Pick where you want to work and try to get a job there. If you don't get a job there, get a job somewhere else, and keep trying at the place you really want to work. I can't tell you how many people have told me they've hired people because they just wanted them to stop calling. But show us the love. We want that passion.

When you come to interview, tell the editor everything you're going to be able to do for them on the Web. Be knowledgeable about the Web site as well as the magazine.

And use every connection that you have. It's only a meritocracy once you have a job, and it's not even necessarily a meritocracy then. People stupider than you and less talented will get promoted while you're still opening mail. When I was at *Rolling Stone*, my editor's other assistant was Jane Pratt. I found out that it was actually my boss who had recommended her to go to *Sassy*. This practically killed me. She got a television show, had a magazine named after her, and she knew Michael Stipe, and I was still slaving away assigning features somewhere. I'm actually okay with the way my life turned out, and I think she's happy with the way her life turned out, but at the time, I thought that we were at least *equally* talented.

And what should you do once you get the job? Read. Watch. Listen. Be the person who knows the most about whatever it is that you're interested in. When you pitch a story to your editors, know what the headline is, what the cover line is, and what the art will be.

And volunteer for everything. Researching, reporting, standing in the press line in freezing rain to get a quote from someone, writing for the Web site, editing the letters page, corresponding with readers. Be enthusiastic, be humble. You may be smarter than I am—you probably are—but you don't know more about what my job requires than I do. Yet.

4

Editing a Thought-Leader Magazine

Michael Kelly (1957–2003), an editor and award-winning reporter, was editor-at-large for *The Atlantic Monthly* and a syndicated columnist for *The Washington Post*. He began his writing career in 1983 as a reporter for *The Cincinnati Post*, and later, the *Baltimore Sun*. Between 1989 and 1992, he was a freelance writer for *The Boston Globe*, *GQ*, *Esquire*, and *The New Republic*. He joined *The New York Times* in 1992, first as a political reporter and later as a writer for *The New York Times Magazine*. His 1992 book about his experiences in the Gulf War, *Martyr's Day: Chronicle of a Small War*, won the PEN-Martha Albrand award. Kelly edited and reported on foreign and political affairs for *The New Yorker* until 1996, when he was appointed editor for *The New Republic*. In 1997, he became a columnist for *National Journal* and a syndicated columnist for *The Washington Post*. In 1998, he became editor of *National Journal*, and in 2000, of *The Atlantic Monthly*, where he was appointed editor-at-large in 2002. Michael Kelly died in 2003 in Iraq while covering the war. His lecture was given on February 7, 2002.

I want to begin with a small story that reflects poorly upon myself. When I was beginning to freelance just before the Gulf War, and was very broke, I got a terrific windfall. I was living in Chicago, off my girlfriend's earnings—I was making about $2,000 to $3,000 a year—when I met an editor from *Playboy*. *Playboy* was based—I guess still is based—in Chicago, so I had a chat with him, and to my astonishment got an assignment worth $5,000 or $6,000.

It was at least double my annual income. The assignment was to go around the country and write about sex in America. And it was understood at the beginning, this being *Playboy*, that it would be generally a positive article, upbeat and so on.

And that was okay by me. I didn't have any strong feelings about it one way or the other. So for a couple of months I went all around the country—*Playboy* had a lot of money, and this was a subject dear to their heart, so they would okay any expense—and watched people make blue movies, and went to all sorts of clubs, straight clubs and gay clubs and swingers' clubs and S&M clubs and so on. And the more I did it, the more depressed I got, because the world I was wandering in seemed, at least to me, a rather grim place filled with grim, sad men, pathetic really, engaged in a kind of dismal and pathetic pursuit.

But it was the first time I had ever gotten material that I thought could be written up at length in a descriptive fashion, which was the kind of writing I wanted to do. So I really worked at the writing and wrote this long, bleak, despairing, grim, sordid story of sex in America, mostly focusing on the god-awful wretchedness of all the men out there that I was taking notes on.

And then I handed it in to my editor, and he called me in a few days later for lunch and he said, "This is really a nice piece of writing. You really captured something here, and you've really got down on paper the sheer awfulness of these guys' lives, how sad and lonely and pathetic they are." And I said, "Thank you very much."

He said, "Here at *Playboy* we have a term for those men." And I said, "Really?" He said, "Yes, we call them our readers."

He rejected the piece, and I would like to stand here and tell you that I stood on the principle of my art and pocketed the kill fee. But I really needed all the money, so I took the piece home and rewrote it, and in the end it turned out to be upbeat and positive and cheerful. I still have the original somewhere, and maybe I'll get it published one of these days, but it taught me a lesson—that I sort of absorbed at the time and sort of didn't—about what magazines were and how they were different from the world I had come from, the newspaper world. (I'd been a newspaper reporter for about twelve years before that.)

What that taught me begins with the notion that any magazine is, in the end, what a very small, self-selected group of people—its readers—wants it to be. And the magazine is shaped to that. It may not be shaped to that explicitly when the magazine starts and defines itself, but it is shaped like that along the way. And in this way, magazines assume what becomes almost an organic form, which is very hard to change.

What I want to talk about tonight are three types of form, and where they fit in with journalism in general. And this begins with an understanding of where journalism fits in with reality in general.

Reality has two salient qualities. The first is that it's real. The second is that it's a mess. It is absolutely chaotic. It is not weighted in any organized fashion. It is just a kind of ongoing wreck every day. This is our lives, this is the world around you.

Journalism has two related salient qualities. It's not real—it is artificial, like all storytelling. And it's orderly. It is designed, in fact, to take the daily wreck, the chaos and the mess out there, and impose upon it a false order.

There is a book that I read a couple of years ago, a small, odd book called *News and the Culture of Lying*, by Paul Weaver. And in this he argued that the basic structure of journalism is by necessity, by definition, a lie.

He was writing from a polemical point of view, and "lie" is a harsh word—I'm not sure I would use it, because of its connotations—but his essential point is right. What he was saying is that the reporter gets up in the morning and he goes out and looks at the world around him and has a certain assignment to look at a certain aspect of the world.

But what the reporter sees is this chaos, this disorganized, highly ambiguous, self-conflicting mess. But by 4 p.m. or 5 p.m., in an a.m. cycle, the reporter has to render that into some sort of order. It is not permissible to come back to an editor at 4 p.m. and say that as far as you can tell, what happened today was an ambiguous mess. I know this because

I was, in many ways, a bad reporter and I've actually tried this, and it does not work.

Nor does it work if you go to your editors at 4 p.m. and argue for a vision of the world that you have organized in your head and that doesn't comport with any known sense of reality that they're familiar with.

What editors want is to have that chaos organized in a fashion that can be presented in a periodical publication. All periodical publications are similarly engaged in this artifice: *The New York Times* tells you every day that it contains all the news that is fit to print, and we all know that isn't true. It can't be true. But to *The New York Times*' credit, they're out there with the artifice telling you on the front page, "This is what you're buying here." You are buying an organizing principle. The world is full of stuff that happened yesterday, much of which is unknown, much of which no one can make any sense out of. But this thing you hold in your hands attempts to make some sense out of it. And of course, dismally fails, as all journalistic analysis ultimately fails, but it at least gives you the comfort of a kind of organization to impose on it.

What journalism does, beyond imposing sheer order, is to impart a worldview. Newspapers do this in a more implicit fashion than magazines, partly because they cover so much more.

A newspaper like the *Times* makes some real effort every day to give you a sense of a great deal of what happens in the world, as opposed to a magazine, which is much more narrow in its focus. In part that's because of the doctrine of objectivity, which works both to good and to ill in truthtelling. Objectivity means that the newspaper is not going to explicitly tell you how to think about the world. But then, we all know that the *New York Post* and *The New York Times* have two very different views of how to look at the world, even if what they publish is presented as an objective view of what happened yesterday. It is not only ordered and weighted to tell you what's important, it's ordered and weighted to comport with a certain worldview.

Still, for all of that, newspapers are more catholic, broader, and less explicit in their worldviews than magazines are. The reason for this gets back to my dismal experience with *Playboy*. Magazines do not even attempt the pretense of looking at all the world. The magazine constructs a world within the larger world, a slice of the world, a viewpoint, and there are different ways you can do this. It can be simply subject matter. This is a magazine about cooking pasta. That's all it is. This is a magazine for cat fanciers; that's all it is. But it can be much more than that and much more complicated than that.

Turning now more directly to magazines, I want to talk about three kinds of magazines—using as examples magazines that I've worked on—and take them in order of explicitness and narrowness.

The first group would be magazines in which the worldview is arranged implicitly. There is no pretense of universal coverage and there's much less of a pretense of objectivity, although there is still some adhering to it. A magazine of this type would be, for instance, *The New Yorker*, *The New York Times Magazine*, or the magazine I currently edit, *The Atlantic Monthly*. These are magazines that call themselves general-interest magazines and, like a newspaper, are broad enough (in theory) to look at anything that happens in the world.

Magazines of this sort do not tell you what to think about the world. They don't tell you that they have a political view or an ideological view upfront. They are explicitly not explicit. But their great purpose, beyond simply entertaining people or presenting to people interesting new stories, is to offer a group of people who wants to look at the world in a certain way a publication that very consistently, even rigidly, offers that view back to them.

They are a kind of a comfort magazine. If you are the sort of person who wants to think of himself or herself as a *New Yorker* reader, *The New Yorker* is not going to savage that belief. You are not going to pick up *The New Yorker* and suddenly find that it seems to have been written for a *Guns & Ammo* reader. It is going to remain written for you. It is going to remain true to a very well-understood sensibility that it's pitched at, which is, if you're a longtime subscriber, your sensibility.

I think anybody who works at *The New Yorker* or *The Atlantic Monthly* could tell you what those magazines stand for. On the wall outside my office in Boston, I have a list of ten guiding rules that one of the previous editors wrote down, some thirty or forty years ago, to guide future editors, and one of them—number eight, I think—is that *The Atlantic* is a liberal magazine, period.

And that does not mean that *The Atlantic* is explicitly political or explicitly ideological, but it is progressive. It has been for nearly 150 years, largely in the sense of progressing the national conversation. But that is in itself a liberal viewpoint.

A last example of this kind of magazine is *The Economist,* even if in structure, it looks like a different kind of magazine completely. *The Economist* looks like a newsmagazine for a rarefied audience, for people who want much more substance, much more in the way of facts than they can get from *Time* or *Newsweek,* and also want a specific kind of substance that they can't get from *Time* or *Newsweek,* which is financial news in depth. *The Economist* gives them long, tedious articles about the gross national product of places that you are never going to go to (and if you're like me, you only have a dim grasp of what a gross national product is).

Not everybody, to put it mildly, who gets *The Economist* actually reads the whole thing. I think a lot of *Economist* subscribers read about six or seven pages in it. I'm sure that nobody reads those 30-page special sections that they run. Yet *The Economist* has a 7 to 10 percent annual growth rate in this country and about a 90 percent renewal rate for a subscription that is over $100, so it's a phenomenally popular magazine.

People get *The Economist*—and this is why *The Economist* belongs with *The Atlantic* and *The New Yorker*—because it does the same thing that *The Atlantic* and *The New Yorker* do. It tells you implicitly how to look at the world in a certain way. *The Economist* stands for free markets. It stands for pro-Americanism. It stands for business. It stands for capitalism. It stands for an old-fashioned kind of liberalism that most people would now think of as Toryism. And its job is not just to package the weekly events of the world in a different factual way than *Time* and *Newsweek* do and with more substance. It's to package it along these lines for people who, consciously or not, want the world organized along these lines.

That's the first group, the category with implicit boundaries. Next in my categorization are a much smaller group of magazines, where the boundaries are explicit, and these are the openly partisan or political or ideological magazines. *The Nation*, obviously, is one. The magazine that I used to edit, *The New Republic*, is another one, and there are others—*National Review* and *The Weekly Standard* on the right, and so on.

There's not very many of them, and none of them has very many subscribers. The marketplace for explicitly political magazines in this country—probably in all countries—is quite small. But they are of great interest to students of magazines for a number of reasons, the principal one being that these magazines have tremendous influence.

The reason for this is that they don't ever pretend to the myth of objectivity. They explicitly say to you, "There is a way of looking at the world that is *right*, and we represent this, and we are going to tell you what fits in with this and what doesn't, and when you pick us up, that's what you are buying."

The Weekly Standard, which is a conservative magazine in Washington, is rigorous about writing about the events of the current week. It has immense value for the political reader like myself, because you can pick it up on a Friday and in a thirty-minute read, it plugs all of the important political events of that week into this matrix. And if you want to know what a certain camp of conservatives think about whatever happened this week, it's going to tell you that, and you're going to know how to think about it. That's what these magazines do.

This explicitness tremendously limits their size, because for every one potential reader who agrees with the ideology of the magazine, there's a much larger group that doesn't. These magazines suffer, also, from a narrowness. It's very easy for a magazine like this to become orthodox or muscle-bound in its views, because when you are explicit about your parameters it is hard to get away with any deviationism.

I know this because I tried to deviate at *The New Republic* for ten months before finding out that it absolutely did not work, that these magazines only exist for the people who cherish them for their explicitness, and I suppose they will never have a moneymaking place in the range of magazines. But their power and influence is surprisingly large precisely because of the odd virtue of explicitness and narrowness.

The third group that interests me is a kind of a magazine that in a sense eschews worldview, because it's going so far down the spectrum toward narrowness that all it does is present just-the-facts reporting about a very, very small world.

These are niche publications, really—or business-to-business publications—where the world is small but where there is immense value to that small group of readers who are therefore willing to pay a lot for it. They don't need an organizing principle such as *The Economist* or *The New Yorker* or *The Atlantic* gives them implicitly. They don't need a polemical set of boundaries such as *The New Republic* or *The Nation* gives them. They just need this very, very small world described through an exhaustive level of reporting that they can't get elsewhere.

I picked up one such magazine a couple of days ago by chance, when waiting in a doctor's office—a magazine for professional restaurateurs and restaurant chefs. You can't imagine anything less worth reading for those of us who are not restaurateurs or chefs. There was nothing there at all, but it cost $5, which is a healthy price for an issue, and without knowing its economics, I am sure that it's every bit as much a money-maker as *The Atlantic* is not. People who need the information that this little publication is going to give them need it a great deal, and they would pay not $5 but $25 for it.

The lead story of the issue I picked up was a 900-word profile of the new global president for McDonald's. *The Wall Street Journal* gave that same job appointment a paragraph, and *The New York Times* business section probably gave it a line.

The company that I worked with before coming to *The Atlantic* owned a number of these publications, so I'm very familiar with their economics. It all comes down to an inverse relationship between narrowness and value, which seems perverse, but it's very real. *National Journal*, which I edited for a couple of years, is a magazine for people who are professionally involved in politics and policy. About a quarter of the subscribers are in government, usually on a fairly high level. Another quarter are in journalism. Another quarter are K Street lobbyists, lawyers, trade group representatives, and so on, and another quarter are academics, but they are all professionally involved in politics and policy, and they are all, of course, institutional customers. None of them is actually paying for the subscription out of their pocket. Their university or newspaper or law firm is paying for it.

National Journal has, I think, about 5,000 subscribers. The current annual subscription price is $1,500 a year, and we are thinking of raising it to $2,000. There probably won't be any price resistance to raising it from $1,500 to $2,000. There was none when it was raised from $1,100 to $1,500. The magazine takes in so much money with that price point, and with about double or triple the ad pages that *New Republic* has, that it can afford an editorial staff of 37 full-time employees.

The *National Journal* has more people covering Capitol Hill than *The New York Times*, the *L.A. Times*, and *The Boston Globe* combined. I think they have twenty people on the Hill on any given day. It covers agencies no one else covers and hearings no one else even goes near. It covers all of that, year in and year out, because that's what the little group of people who pay a great deal of money for it actually wants. And they want it without any explicit worldview presented to them—they don't even want much of an implicit worldview. For this kind of publication, the closer you can get to affectlessness, the better. In the *National Journal*'s case, for instance, roughly half of the readers are Republican and half are Democratic. When the administration changes or when control of the House of Representatives changes, the magazine has to be able to stay in business. If it was even remotely suspected of skewing, even implicitly, to one side or another, it would lose ground very quickly. The same is true for any trade publication.

Yet when you think about the point I started out with, that all magazines exist to shape the chaotic world in an artificial, organized way, which is more narrow and focused than what a newspaper does—that's still true even in this extreme example, because the shaping here is done entirely by weight and narrowness.

Again taking the example of *National Journal*, what *National Journal* in effect says to readers is, "Here is a publication of some fifty edit pages a week, and it doesn't cover anything—anything—that happens in the world except stuff that happened in politics, in policy, inside the Beltway."

That's the whole world. There is no other world out there. It doesn't even pretend to be interested in anything else. If you only read *National Journal* for a year, you'd not only not know what the current movies were, you might not know movies existed.

Well, that is not just order, that's worldview. The same is true of the publication of the restaurant association. Although there isn't even an implicit worldview attached to it, by its sheer exclusionary nature it is saying to readers that this is the whole world there is.

Not surprisingly, this is the easiest kind of magazine to make money on. Anybody considering the insane notion of starting a new magazine first looks at a niche publication. Because it is the only kind of publication where you can actually see yourself making money with a very small group of subscribers who pay a great deal and with advertisers who will pay a great deal to reach those subscribers, precisely because you've made yourself so narrow.

It occurred to me, when I was writing this down, that it all might sound quite depressing, that the end result of this is a message that magazines are spectacularly uncreative things. That even to financially fail at a magazine but remain publishing, you have to conduct yourself within these narrow confines.

I actually think that the opposite is true, as long as you understand the structure of the business underneath you. I think that the structure actually allows you boundless creativity precisely because what the structure says to you is, yes, a magazine has to pitch itself at a certain world and pitch itself over and over and over again to that world, to a degree that at many magazines reaches a level of insanity. Anybody who looks at any of the main women's or men's magazines knows that they are the same publications over and over, with the same articles every month.

And that is the obvious drawback of this reality. But the same reality means that—again, if you understand it, and if you don't try to deny it, or to make something that violates the natural rules of the form—you can make whatever you want.

You could tomorrow start any magazine on any subject that you can think of, and in theory have it be successful, if you can just say to yourself,

We're making a magazine for people who care about this and that's all we are doing; we're pitching it at them; we're going to create a world for them that doesn't exist right now, and if we get X number of them to pay Y amount of money, we can do whatever we want. We're free of advertisers, concerns, we're free of anything. We can make within this rigidity anything we want and actually make it work. And despite all that you hear about the dismal state of the magazine business (which is all true), magazines do this all the time. And the ones that are successful do it by understanding the structure.

One of my favorite magazines is a magazine that is published in Boston called *Cook's Illustrated*. It's different from all the other food magazines in a very basic way. The other food magazines are—as Nora Ephron pointed out many years ago—really a sort of soft porn of food. The point, in the end, of *Gourmet* magazine is to look at the center spread, but at just a pot roast. And they all have various differences—editorial design is one—but they are essentially competing in that same territory.

Cook's Illustrated was founded in 1980 by Christopher Kimball, who looked at the world of people who cared a lot about food and recognized that there wasn't a publication for people who were not interested in the soft-porn aspect of food but actually wanted to know how to cook a pot roast, and who wanted to know how to cook it on a given Saturday if they lived in Des Moines.

For *Cook's Illustrated*, you didn't have to live in Manhattan and have access to exotic ingredients. They knew that if they made a magazine that in each issue just told people who really liked to cook how to cook five or six things perfectly—the best pot roast, the best roast chicken, the best apple pie—if they did that and delivered on that promise, they would get a passionate audience.

In their business plan creating this magazine—for which there was no known model, and which most magazine consultants would tell them was a very bad idea because it could not hope to attract advertising the way *Gourmet* and the big magazines did—they posited financial success with a magazine that would be printed on relatively cheap paper, would have a low editorial overhead and a small staff. But they insisted that the magazine would adhere to the highest editorial standards—very good editing, very good writing—and what they set out to do, they would do better than anybody else has ever tried. And with zero advertising, they knew they would start making money if they got 50,000 subscribers.

They now have 350,000 subscribers. The four founders are all obscenely rich. The magazine still has no advertising, and has none of the headaches associated with advertising. It has none of the headaches associated with almost all of the business side of the magazine industry—direct mail, any of that. None of that exists for them. They have a 97 percent renewal rate. And they are so beloved by their readers that at the beginning of each subscription year, they offer subscribers the chance to buy the magazine twice. You can subscribe to it for the year, and you can also check a box which will allow you to pay double and at the end of the year they'll send you all the magazines that you've already got, but in a box, bound.

Fifty percent of their subscribers check that box and pay for the magazine twice. And at the same time they're having this spectacular financial success, they have achieved a level of editorial integrity and independence that is unheard of in the magazine industry at large, and they have done that basically by understanding the structure that a magazine has to live in, a structure that gives, in fact, a great deal of freedom. As long as you acknowledge it's there.

5

Fact-Checking at *The New Yorker*

Peter Canby is a senior editor and the head of the fact-checking department at *The New Yorker*. He wrote *The Heart of the Sky: Travels Among the Maya* (1992) and numerous magazine stories. His lecture was delivered on February 28, 2002.

When I first interviewed to join the checking department a number of years ago, the then managing editor of *The New Yorker* told me that fact-checking was the best way to learn the basics of journalism, much better than a journalism degree, he assured me.

The New Yorker has traditionally devoted a lot of resources to its fact-checking department. There are presently sixteen fact-checkers. To many people that sounds like a lot, but there are no assistant or associate editors at *The New Yorker* and in many ways checkers, along with the top-level copyeditors, fill that gap.

The role that a checker plays at *The New Yorker* ranges from completely simple, like getting names and dates right, to extraordinarily challenging. New checkers usually work first on simple stories in which they do just that: they get the names and dates right. Which is not as simple as it sounds. Rather than go into the details of how you know when you've hit a correct spelling of a name or what a correct date is, I will just say that I think it is probably analogous to that central reportorial skill of knowing when you've got something right. And it's not easy because there's a lot of information out there, and a lot of it is wrong.

We always break in new checkers on manageable pieces—"Talk" stories, book and movie reviews—but even that isn't always easy. In the bad old days of *The New Yorker*, when I started, we had a film reviewer who was a bit of a narcoleptic; she once fell asleep during a movie screening and ran two movies together, and it was very challenging to try to straighten the plots out.

But soon after checkers get through that initial stage, they move on to more complicated pieces, and eventually they start working on pieces that are being checked and edited and written all at the same time. In these situations, the editor is quite often buried under trying to make narrative sense out of a piece that is really a breaking story, and the checker becomes the person in the magazine who kind of stands outside the piece and becomes central to closing and editing it.

So what is the purpose of the fact-checking department? The basic purpose, of course, is to prevent errors from appearing in the magazine. Checking, of course, also has an important legal rationale, and we work very closely with *The New Yorker*'s lawyer. But I want to argue that the ultimate benefit of fact-checking, if not its ultimate purpose, is something more complicated.

All of you who have done research on whatever topic will no doubt recognize that facts tend to perpetuate themselves. Reference books source other reference books, histories are written on secondary sources, until in many books the original fact and the original situation become completely occluded and distant. And you learn to recognize how narratives based on this kind of research have a certain unoriginal quality.

You can call it a subset of the Stephen Ambrose syndrome, but to me original research has a freshness that recycled knowledge doesn't. And I would say that writers who have grappled with original issues or have done original reporting, or have looked at something with a really fresh eye, achieve a distinctive texture in their writing. And while no one brings that to the writing but the writer, the checking department attempts to ask really critical questions, to look at logic, at the flaws in arguments, and to try to get these things addressed so that what ultimately appears in the magazine does have this texture of freshness and originality and accuracy. This not only gives the magazine its credibility but also imparts a distinctive quality to *The New Yorker* prose. So you're hearing it here first, the fact-checking theory of lit crit.

Preventing errors from appearing in the magazine is not a simple process. For openers, you need to know that in addition to the basic reporting pieces, we also check "The Talk of the Town," the critics, fiction, poetry, cartoons, art, captions, the table of contents, certain of the several-paragraph-long essays in the "Goings On" section. We also fact-check the contributors page, the cover wrap, the letters column, all the press releases, and a good deal of the recently mounted Web site.

To start checking a nonfiction piece, you begin by consulting the writer about how the piece was put together and using the writer's sources as well as our own departmental sources. We then essentially take the piece apart and put it back together again. You make sure that the names and dates are right, but then if it is a John McPhee piece, you make sure that the USGS report that he read, he read correctly; or if it is a John le Carré piece, when he says his con man father ran for Parliament in 1950, you make sure that it wasn't 1949 or 1951.

Or if we describe the basis on which the FDA approved or disapproved the medical tests that ImClone used for Erbitux, then you need to find out what the complexities of that whole situation were. And of course, this kind of thing has consequences, because if you get it wrong, it matters. We also work on complicated pieces such as the ones we've been running this fall about the Pentagon's top-secret team that is trained to snatch nukes away from belligerent countries, or the piece about the Predator drone that had a clear shot at Mullah Omar, for better or for worse, and didn't take the shot because the CENTCOM attorneys were not clear on the legality of that operation.

And these stories have an impact. I'm told that the last story in particular drove Secretary of Defense Rumsfeld crazy when we published it.

But the unfortunate thing is that when *The New Yorker* is wrong on these allegations, which we are from time to time, the cry goes out not for the writer or for the editor but for the fact-checker. In the department, we refer to that as the Shoot-the-Fact-Checker Syndrome, which is one of our occupational hazards.

Prior to the Tina Brown period, there were eight checkers. And particularly during the editorship of William Shawn, which was when I started—Shawn was the editor of *The New Yorker* from '52 to '87—stories progressed in an orderly, almost stately way toward publication. Writers would work on pieces for as long as they felt was useful and necessary, and that often meant years. Once the pieces were accepted, they were edited, copyedited, and fact-checked on a schedule that typically stretched out for weeks and sometimes for months.

This process could produce some really wonderful writing. The last piece I worked on before I left *The New Yorker* the first time around was something that I always think epitomizes a Shawn-era piece, although it was published by Shawn's distinguished successor, Bob Gottlieb. But I think it was commissioned by Shawn. This piece was *The New Yorker*'s four-part excerpt of Neil Sheehan's *A Bright Shining Lie*, which is a Vietnam book that went on to win not only a National Book Award but also a Pulitzer Prize.

Sheehan was one of the top Vietnam journalists. He was the reporter to whom Daniel Ellsberg gave the Pentagon Papers. The subject of *A Bright Shining Lie* was a man named John Paul Vann. Sheehan had met Vann in the early '60s when he was a UPI reporter in Vietnam and Vann was a kind of maverick army officer who was very critical of the way that the world was being conducted even then.

Not only a maverick but also a loose cannon—he talked readily to the press, and he was a source for a number of the early journalists. But Vann increasingly became a strident dissident voice within the military, which did not make the military happy. Eventually he alienated himself from the army command and left the army in disgrace. But due to a peculiar genius that this character had, he returned to Vietnam as a civilian and became the number three person in command of the Vietnam War after the ambassador and the commander-in-chief, which I think is completely unprecedented in American military history.

He was eventually killed. It was typical of him that even in this elevated position, he was involved in a battle and had to escape by helicopter. The helicopter got shot down, and he was killed. After his death he became an obsession for Sheehan, who had worked on the book about him, *A Bright Shining Lie*, for sixteen years.

Another checker and I spent two months working on *The New Yorker* excerpts of *A Bright Shining Lie*. It was made particularly difficult because Sheehan lived near Washington and he had his sources for this book in twenty-five army-surplus file cabinets lined up in a special room in his house. And these were not little Door Store file cabinets, these were heavy industrial file cabinets that stretched a good three or four feet back to the wall, and they weren't filled up with fat reports but with single sheets of paper. This was sixteen years of work, and it was really out of the question for him to send this stuff to New York, so we went to Washington. Then life got more complicated because Sheehan is an insomniac and he didn't get up till three in the afternoon every day. So we had to adjust our schedules to that.

But it was a completely brilliant piece, and I think it is a perfect example of the kind of thing I was talking about before, the quality of writing that is so densely researched. It clings so closely to the strangeness of the world that we all live in, or certainly the world that John Paul Vann lived in, that it had this really refreshing, original quality and it contained all the moral ambivalence of its subject, John Paul Vann.

And despite winning a Pulitzer Prize and a National Book Award, which means that it has to have sold well, it still could not have been a commercial proposition, because it took sixteen years to produce. I want to point out to those of you who aspire to producing really memorable things that it requires a lot of time and patience and a belief in yourself, when professional logic tells you to hurry up and turn things around every two or three weeks.

One more thing I want to say about Neil Sheehan is that it was a particularly frustrating experience for us fact-checkers because Neil Sheehan never got anything wrong, and at the end of two months we would go, "Neil, give us a break, you know? Give us one little thing we can change." If every writer were like this, the checking department would be a complete waste of time, but it is really to Neil Sheehan's credit that he was like this.

I can't leave the subject of the Shawn-era *New Yorker* without at least one more story that illustrates a completely different aspect of the old magazine, and this was its tendency to warehouse complicated fact pieces. There was an inventory sheet that went around every week, of fact pieces, and I think it was 100 pieces long. And considering that each of these pieces was worth $10,000 or $20,000 to the magazine, that was a lot of inventory.

One of these bottom dwellers had been in house for many years. It showed no signs of running, but I took a liking to it. It was called "A Scottish Childhood." I can't remember the name of the author, but it was a woman who had grown up in a drafty little castle in the Highlands of Scotland, and when her father died, her oldest brother inherited everything through primogeniture.

She was essentially, sort of in a gentle way, disinherited. She went to London. She wrote a memoir about growing up in this delightful and strange environment and she sold it. She sold it in *The New Yorker* as a work of fiction, but it was thinly fictionalized. By the time I latched onto this piece, it had become a fact piece and showed no signs of ever getting published.

But one day it kicked up on the schedule. So I was able to call the woman in London and say that the piece that you sold twenty years ago is going to press tomorrow or something. In the meantime she had gotten married. She'd had a child. The child had grown up and the child had gotten married and divorced—so long was this piece in house. And it was really a delightful piece, and though perhaps for her not worth the wait, she didn't miss a beat when I called her.

So that was the old *New Yorker*. The biggest difference between David Remnick's *New Yorker* today and the Shawn *New Yorker* is timeliness. During the Shawn years, book reviews ran months, even years out of sync with publication dates. Writers wrote about major issues without any concern for news pegs or what was going on in the outside world.

That was the way people thought, and it was really the way the whole editorial staff was tuned.

All this changed when Tina Brown arrived. Whereas before, editorial schedules were predictable for weeks or a month in advance, under Tina we began getting 8,000-, 10,000-, 12,000-word pieces in on a Thursday that were to close the following Wednesday. But something else changed in a way that is more important. Prior to Tina, the magazine really had been writer-driven, and I think this is why they gave the writers so much liberty. They wanted the writers to develop their own, often eccentric, interests.

Under Tina, writing concepts began to originate in editors' meetings, and assignments were given out to writers who were essentially told what to write. And a lot of what the editors wanted was designed to be timely and of the moment and tended to change from day to day. So the result was that we were working on pieces that were really much more controversial and much less well-formulated than anything we had dealt with previously, and often we would put teams of checkers to work on these pieces and checking and editing could go on all night.

I would also say that there is no point in mythologizing the past. While there were many brilliant pieces in the old *New Yorker*, there were also some crashingly boring pieces, but we won't go into that. But by focusing the magazine on the present, Tina really did, to her credit, liberate it in many ways, and she really set the stage for David Remnick, our present editor. She set the table for David, who has done a great job combining some of the eccentricities and some of the humor and some of the streetwise tone of the old *New Yorker* with the timeliness that Tina set the precedent for.

So *The New Yorker* now is—in my opinion—in better shape than it's been in for years. But what has all this meant for fact-checking and its role in the magazine?

The problem for us moving into *The New Yorker*'s timely era was to figure out how to apply the same standards of checking that we had applied to Shawn and Gottlieb's magazine. And the first thing that happened is that we doubled the number of checkers to sixteen, and then we got desktop LexisNexis for all the checkers. I'm sure that you're all familiar with Nexis. It is incredibly expensive, but kind of indispensable. Once you start using it, you can't not use it. But it has great perils, and I can think of no better example than when I was working with a new checker who was doing a cigarette story, and Philip Morris came up. I said, "Why don't you try out how to spell Philip Morris in Nexis?" and she plugged in a spelling of Philip Morris with two Ls that kicked up 130 stories or something, which, if you weren't thinking about it, would basically confirm that you were right. But if you check the correct one-L spelling, it'll tell you the search has been interrupted because there are more than a thousand entries. In other words, there are 130 people who've misspelled Philip Morris in the recent past, and if you don't use Nexis critically you're just going to go and parrot the mistake that somebody else has made.

We find all kinds of things through Nexis, but almost the most useful thing that it does is allow us to frame the debate around the story, so that if we want to know what other people are saying about the subject and what the issues are, it's not that hard. If you have a spare hour you can go compile a major paper file and just read, and then you can go in and get the details you need in different ways, using more reliable sources than Nexis.

When the new, remade *The New Yorker* of the last decade was gearing up and we started getting all these late-breaking stories, issues such as logic and fairness and balance—which previously had been the responsibility of the editors—began to fall on the checkers. This wasn't by anybody's design. It was because the editors were really busy putting these stories together and they wanted us to look at things from the outside and see how they were framed, and look at them from the inside and look at the logic and the way they were reported and the way quotes were used and many other such things.

That responsibility came to us not in the way of anybody saying suddenly, "You're doing that." It just became that when a problem arose, they would come to us and say, "Why didn't you warn us?" And so it just became clear that there was this gap between editing and checking that had opened up under the pressure of later-breaking stories, and it just seemed logical that we should fill it. It made our job more challenging, and more fun.

Another change that took place in *The New Yorker* fact-checking during this same period came about in the mid-'90s as the result of the fallout from what was known as the Janet Malcolm case. Janet Malcolm is a *New Yorker* writer of great distinction. In 1983, she wrote a profile of a psychoanalyst named Jeffrey Masson, who subsequently sued her and the magazine for libel (it was an unfavorable story).

The court case didn't resolve itself until 1994. The charge was that Janet Malcolm had compressed, rearranged, and even fabricated quotes. In 1993, *The New Yorker* was separated out of the judgment and in 1994, Malcolm was cleared of libel charges in the U.S. District Court in San Francisco. Prior to this resolution, when writers gave us their sources, they gave us books, magazine clips, news clips, and phone numbers, but they didn't give us notes, and after the resolution of the case, we began to insist that writers turn in their notes to us as well.

And prior to the case, when people were quoted, we would call them up and we'd go over the information in the quote, but we would never go over the quote with them, for obvious reasons. You go over a quote with somebody, they don't like the way they sound. Even if they said something, they are going to say, "Oh, that's not what I meant." Then there's a problem. So that standard still holds. When we call people on the phone, which we do all the time, we never read them their quotes.

But after the Malcolm case was settled, we began to ask writers to include their notes, their tapes, and their transcripts with their source material, and this gave us a great deal more flexibility in how to approach stories. We continued to call sources, as I mentioned, but whenever there was a particularly controversial or sensitive issue or it was somebody that we couldn't reach for whatever reason, we had the notes to fall back on. And the ideal for us—in fact, pretty much the norm—is both to use the notes and to call people, because notes can be wrong, just as with everything else.

And we always did the best we could to give people who were mentioned in a piece the chance to let us know if there was some wild-card reason not to publish the piece. It also allowed us the courtesy of telling people that they were about to appear in *The New Yorker*, so they wouldn't be hit completely out of the blue. I feel strongly about this, because whether you're delivering them good or bad news, the contact with these ultimately real people humanizes the process. I often think of the fact-checking process as setting off a series of controlled explosions, where it's much better to have people go off before publication than afterward.

The use of writers' notes raised another set of complicated issues. At the inception of this policy there was a lot of internal debate about how to go about it, and the suggestion was made that we require writers to use tape recorders. And this was rejected because of the general feeling that we didn't want to put writers in a methodological straitjacket. But the result of that is that we got notes in all shapes and sizes, ranging from completely clear and legible and word-processed to the completely illegible.

Sometimes writers presented what were clearly second-generation notes. One long-term Shawn-era writer who didn't like the change in procedures gave us for several stories a notebook filled with scrawls—you could picture her at home going, "Ha ha ha." She got over that eventually.

All this put us in danger, however, of appearing like thought police, and it required on the part of the checkers a great deal of diplomacy and, where appropriate, firmness. Obviously, a reporter's notes are sacred to that reporter, and reporters typically don't share their notes with anybody. So imagine you're a high-level reporter for the *Times* or *The Washington Post* and you are suddenly asked to turn over your notes, not by some federal court who is threatening to put you in prison but by a fact-checker who is threatening to put you in prison.

Most of the complications surrounding the new policy revolved around the question of how we would use notes. When you actually report something, you're sitting and talking with somebody. If you're writing it by hand, it's really not possible to write as quickly as somebody speaks to you. So you don't actually write down what somebody says, you write down a distillation of what somebody says.

You might write keywords, key phrases, sentence fragments. You also know that when you're writing down what somebody says to you,

you have to work with a split mind, probably a three-part mind. You have to be focusing on writing what the person said a few minutes ago. You have to pay attention to what the person is saying in the present, which is different from what you are writing, and you also have to worry about what your next question is going to be.

Then when the interview is done, you put your notebook in your pocket, you put your pen away, you walk out to your car, you do whatever you do, and then the person stops you and says the most important thing of all. And you realize that their saying that at that moment has something to do with the fact that your pen is not in your hand and your notebook is put away, and you realize that if you pull out your notebook and pull out the pen it's going to break the spell and you will wreck this moment of revelation.

So what do you do? You spin the conversation as long as you can get. You get as much as information as you can get, and you go back into your car or hotel room or your coffee shop and you write it down after the fact. And again, that's not exactly what the person said to you, but it's legitimate. This is the way reporting happens.

All of this means that working with someone's notes is not a science. It requires judgment and discretion and a strong sense, which comes only with practice, of what is acceptable and what is not.

Finally there's the question of blind sources, which are really a big part of our work. When we run stories based on blind sources, the checker always gets the notes and always knows who the sources are. Often we speak with the sources, but sometimes we don't. It really depends. If we don't speak with the sources we want a good reason not to, and we want to make sure that all the relevant people inside the magazine realize that so it's a shared decision, not just a fact-checking decision.

But even with all that, there are a number of questions that arise with the use of blind sources, and one is that we try to cite blind sources in a way so that if it's one person, for example, we don't identify that person in three or four different ways, so it sounds like a big swell of opinion. If it's a one-source story, then it should read like a one-source story.

We also make sure that the way people are identified is accurate. We don't want to reveal who it is, but we don't want to mislead the reader.

And we also, of course, go to great lengths to look for on-the-record sources to corroborate information that we get through off-the-record people, but I think that that is the norm in reporting.

We also try to ask ourselves a number of questions about the people we are quoting. We want to think critically, are they in a position to know what they are telling us? And might the person be selectively leaking information to us in order to advance a point of view? At the time of the Whitewater investigation, I was particularly pleased that we killed a Kenneth Starr–sourced item because people inside the magazine realized that we were being manipulated by selective leaks, which is increasingly an element in Washington journalism.

Ultimately we make mistakes. I wish we didn't, but they are inevitable and constant. It does seem to be something of a national sport to write letters to *The New Yorker* and point out these mistakes. And often the mistake letters we receive explain that the letter's writer has been reading *The New Yorker* for years and he's never seen anything like this, that Shawn and Harold Ross must be turning in their graves, that the writer didn't realize that as a cost-cutting measure *The New Yorker* had eliminated its fact-checking department, and did we know that there used to be fact-checkers in the old days?

These letters aren't a great deal of fun for us, but we take some consolation in the idea that the indignation is perhaps a reflection of their high expectations and the degree to which we are generally successful in getting the magazine out there in a fairly sharp and timely fashion.

And the only reason that *The New Yorker* system works, however well it does, is because we've always had very good institutional support. All the editors have been big supporters of the checking process.

And with the help of all these people, fact-checking has become a big part of *The New Yorker*'s editing process, and our end of the bargain is to try to be intelligent and diplomatic. To try to make things work out. To try to not obstruct publication, but to get things as right as they can be, and as right as we can. This doesn't always make us popular inside the magazine, but it seems to work.

6

A Magazine Needs Copyeditors
Because . . .

Barbara Walraff is a contributing editor and the "Word Court" and "Word .
Fugitives" columnist for *The Atlantic Monthly*. She is the author of the nation-
ally best-selling book *Word Court* (2000) as well as *Your Own Words* (2004) and
Word Fugitives (2006). Wallraff is also the editor emeritus of the newsletter
Copy Editor: Language News for the Publishing Profession (now *Copyediting*). Her
many essays on language have appeared in publications including *The New
York Times, The Washington Post, The Boston Globe, The Wilson Quarterly,* and
The New York Times Magazine. Her lecture was delivered March 3, 2006.

I could be a one-woman panel discussion about copyediting. Not only
have I worked as a copyeditor, but I have also worked with copyeditors,
and as an assigning editor and as a writer. I have taught copyeditors, and
the workshops that I taught gave me a chance to listen to the needs and
problems of copyeditors around the country, who work for all types
of publications, everything from professional engineering journals to
Golf Digest.

On the one-woman panel theme, I thought about bringing different
hats to wear and changing them, to show you when I was changing point

of view—copyeditor hat, writer hat, assigning editor hat—but I realized I was just going to end up confusing myself. And I decided it might be better simply to interview myself about copyediting. Then later, you can interview me about anything I left out.

So I brought only one hat to wear when I am the interviewer. And, as myself, I will go hatless.

Q: A magazine needs copyeditors because?
A: Because some writers are not very good at their job. Because writers who are good at their job don't always have the time, given deadlines, to polish their work. And neither do their assigning or supervising editors. Copyeditors spend most of their day, every day, polishing, so they can do this work more efficiently than just about anybody else, and they can always do it in a way that is appropriate to the publication. And the third reason copyeditors are necessary is because even a bunch of highly skilled writers won't do things consistently. And consistency strengthens the identity of a magazine.

If you picked up a copy of *The Atlantic Monthly* and we referred to ourselves in the text sometimes with "the" lower case and sometimes with it capped and ital'd; or if there were a few articles that mentioned Osama Bin Laden and some of them spelled his name Osama, the way most publications do, and some of them spelled it Usama, the way the CIA likes to do it—I don't know about you, but I would start to wonder if anybody on the staff was reading the whole magazine.

So a magazine needs someone, or a team of people, who work on everything and make sure it meets all their standards.

So copyeditors obsess over all of the trivial details. Is that it? No, that's not it. From one point of view, things like capitalization and spelling and punctuation might seem trivial. It might even seem like something that a machine could take care of. So who needs a living, breathing copyeditor?

But turning the job over to a machine wouldn't work, for one thing, because there are no universal English-language standards, or even consistent American English standards, about capitalization and spelling and punctuation and that kind of thing.

So each magazine has to make choices. And every choice you make—do you want to use serial commas or don't you? Do you cap references to officials, like the president?—each choice says a little bit of something about the identity of the magazine. And taken all together, those choices say a lot.

This is a lot like the way a business suit on a man, plus an appropriate shirt, plus a tie, plus dress shoes, tells you something about him. Something slightly different than if he left off the tie and wore loafers. And the impression you would get would be a lot different from what you would see if the same guy were wearing cut-off shorts and a T-shirt.

I am not saying any one outfit is better than another. I am not saying any particular style is inherently bad or good. I am just pointing out that they project different images.

So the way the details add up is not trivial. But they are also not the most important part of the job. I think the most important thing copyeditors do is straighten out tangled, confusing, ungrammatical sentences. And certainly no machine in existence can do anything like that, as I am sure you know, if you have ever turned on the grammar checker on your computer. Word's grammar checker tries, and it's a joke.

Writing is meant to be read by people, and you are a person. As a copyeditor, you are probably the first person to read a piece who is not invested in it beyond that it is going to be part of the magazine.

You are not the writer, who had been asked to write something in particular and did the best he or she could. And you are not the editor who commissioned the piece and has ideas of how what got turned in met the expectations they had or did not meet their expectations. As copyeditor, you probably don't even know what the boss's expectations were for that work.

So you, the copyeditor, are half in the writer's and editor's camp and half in the reader's camp. You are supposed to make the piece be its best self, for all the readers who will come later. And you are supposed to change or flag anything that is going to put later readers off.

So what that means, in practice, depends on who your readers are. Can they read at a college-textbook level? Even if they can, will they be happy to do that?

The answer to that is no, by the way, no matter who your readers are.

Can you make the language simpler, without dumbing down the ideas? What level of general knowledge are your readers presumed to have? For instance, would a first reference to Gregor Mendel read something like, "Gregor Mendel, the nineteenth-century botanist, who founded the science of genetics"? Or do your readers probably already know that, and you should just say, "the geneticist Gregor Mendel"? At a different kind of publication, do you need to ID Coldplay, the popular British band? Or not? Jennifer Lopez or J-Lo? If you are copyediting a music magazine, the answers to those questions would be one thing, and if you are copyediting the AARP magazine, the answers might be different.

Will coarse language offend your readers or titillate them? And how coarse is too coarse for your readers? Everybody has limits. How will the readers feel about slang and jargon? Both kinds of language have their place, but how big a place should they have in your magazine?

So these are some of the standards that copyeditors are supposed to uphold.

Q: Remind me what copyeditors actually do.
A: Well, it varies from one magazine to the next. Workflows vary. And the mechanics of how copyeditors do their job, and how their changes and suggestions get incorporated into manuscript, that all varies.

For my twenty years copyediting at *The Atlantic*, I edited, by hand, on galleys produced by the typesetting department. I gave my marked-up galleys, when I was finished working on them, to the supervising editor, who would discuss the galleys with the writer, if the writer was interested.

Bill Whitworth, the wonderful editor who hired me, during my first week asked me to write little explanations on the galleys of the reasons for my changes, wherever those reasons might not be perfectly obvious to everyone. And he told me that I should always suggest a fix, not just circle something and write "awkward" with a question mark next to it.

And those two directives from Bill turned out to be very important. They helped me be fair-minded, having to explain why I wanted to do something. The explanation just couldn't be "'Cause it sounds better to me." And they helped me win respect.

All the same, the supervising editors were free to cross out any changes they didn't want to make. And then sometimes, when I had pointed out a problem, they would pick a different solution to it than what I had suggested, which was fine with me, as long as the problem got solved.

So the person who is working with the writers has my galleys. Goes over them. And when the two of them are finished, turns my galleys— and also the editor-in-chief's, galleys from the legal department, and that editor's own set of galleys—over to another copyeditor, Martha Spaulding.

Martha was the person I worked with for twenty years. Martha took all these sets of galleys and collated them, writing the changes onto a master set of galleys and looking them over to make sure that everything on all the sets, together, was compatible. That, for instance, the same information wasn't being added in two different places on two different sets of galleys; or that if a section had been cut, that any first references—"Gregor Mendel, the founder of the science of genetics," as opposed to "Mendel," what you would call him on second reference— got transferred to what we kept. And all that kind of thing.

Simultaneously, the fact-checkers were working on the piece. They would put the changes onto the master set themselves. And once they signed off on it, Martha would look at their changes, to make sure they followed the magazine's style and the language was okay.

Typesetters made the revisions; put everything into page format, as specified by the art department; made page groups. And then I reread the piece in page form, which gave me a chance to spot new problems that had been introduced along the line.

And if you are thinking, well, with all that, where could new problems come from?—it happened all the time.

That was also my chance to complain, if there were changes that I had suggested the first time around that hadn't been made, and I thought, *No, that's really important; you've got to do something there.* I got to complain, one last time, before it went off to the printer.

When I started doing all that, it was not anachronistic. It was just unusually careful. By the time I stopped doing it, a few years ago, it was way out of date.

Nowadays, copyeditors tend to work on computer, probably in track-changes mode, so the writer and assigning editor can see what they have done. I actually prefer to work on computer. I turn track changes on and turn off the thing that lets you see what is being changed, so what you are looking at just looks like the changed version. That enables you to read straight through the changed version of the text.

The old way, putting everything in the margins—crossing out a word, putting a new word to replace it in the margin—it required some real mental gyrations in order to figure out what the changed version was going to be like. And you could never see how the writing flowed as well as you can if you just change it on the screen—put the new words right into the text. So count me in favor of the twenty-first century.

Q: If all copyeditors are doing is being helpful, why do they have that reputation?

A: What reputation? Let's see, the charges include that they would try to superimpose their voice on the piece, or change the writer's voice to be theirs, or introduce errors—that they are enemies of creative language. That they are anal and obsessive personalities.

Yes, it's not a very pretty picture in many ways, is it?

A long time ago, I worked at the *Boston Phoenix* weekly newspaper. And we had a new, very pretty, young female copyeditor, who all the guys in the newsroom were just in love with. But the sports guy, who was as much in love with Mimsy as anybody else, was kind of waiting for her to do, you know, those girl things to his sports copy.

And one day, Mimsy, on purpose, pranced by his desk and said, "George, thank you for your latest baseball piece. I knew you didn't want to be incorrect, so I changed RBIs to RsBI." And pranced off.

And George just went nuts. He went stomping in, and somebody said, "George, that was a joke. That was a joke, George. Sit down." And they got along a lot better after that.

The problem with copyediting—and the downside to the job—is that it is a relentlessly negative, critical job. I mean, you try correcting every-body's spelling and grammar and logic and organization, and do that day in, day out, and see how popular that makes you.

If you catch stuff in just about every paragraph, it can be humiliating to the writer and to the supervising editor who's been through it. They may be grateful you notice, but they are going to feel pretty stupid that they didn't.

And if there is something that you didn't catch, or something that you misunderstood and corrected so that it unmistakably said what you thought it said, but it didn't, so now you've made it wrong, and that gets published, then it is only natural for everybody else to feel, well, gee, aren't there any good copyeditors anymore?

So when there is a mistake, people tend to think it is your fault. And when there are no mistakes, they can feel put down by that. So sometimes, copyediting can seem like the most thankless job in the world.

Q: Well, what are some proud moments in your life as a copyeditor?
A: Thank you for asking. Well, one time, we were getting ready to run a major piece on how murder affects the loved ones that the victim leaves behind. This was by a high-profile, very good writer who pays close attention to his language and is not especially eager to be second-guessed.

So when I saw that he called the people who the article was about "murder survivors"—and he did that dozens of times—I thought, *Okay, I am sure he knows that, on the face of it, that is an oxymoron—survivor of murder. But I can't think of any other short phrase to describe the people he is talking about.*

And after a while, "murder survivors"—it does stop jumping off the page at me. But I thought, *Well, all right, why don't I just say what I think, in order to have said it?* And I was fully expecting to be told, "Well, I have thought about it, and thanks."

And what I got back was, "Barbara, I love the way your mind works. Thank you." And he turned every instance of "murder survivors" in the piece to something else. And I was afraid, when I suggested that, that he would find another phrase and just kind of search and replace, and it would come out in a clumsy way. But he didn't. He went through and he changed every reference individually, so that it read smoothly.

I can tell you a bunch of stories like that—kind of "gotcha" stories. The short story where ingrown toenails were actually quite a plot point, but they were referred to as hangnails. And we only found that in the last go—everybody read through it. This man had cherry-red hangnails that required medical attention—and wait a minute, that's not right.

But here is a different kind of proud moment. A really long time ago, when I was working at the *Phoenix*, every time the personal finance columnist would turn in his stuff, I would just grit my teeth, because he was such a terrible writer. I would end up changing something in just about every sentence.

So one day, I was talking to him, and he was talking about something of his that had been published in another publication. And he started complaining, bitterly, about how much they had changed it, how annoying their copyeditor was, and how that person had not done a good job.

And I said something to elicit how he thought that experience was different from his experience with me. And he said, "Well, you just touch up my stuff a little; you don't rewrite everything." And, you know, of course I did.

But I loved that. I mean, that is exactly the goal, to be invisible. And if you can make writers say what they meant better than they did when they said it, or make them say what they would have said if they had thought it forward all the way, and you don't leave any marks of your own, that's being a good copyeditor. And it makes everybody happy. So I was very proud of that.

But, honestly, proud moments are not especially relevant to being a good copyeditor, unfortunately. More relevant is just slogging along. You might get a big piece that obviously has something really important to say to the readers. But when it lands in your in-box, your heart sinks, because there is just page after page of bad writing. So you slog.

And sometimes, it would take me two or three days to do a big piece, just patiently making it better, line by line. Sometimes you think you understand what the writer has in mind here. You get four paragraphs farther on, and you realize, *Oh, no, that isn't what he was saying. I misunderstood it, because he didn't say it well.* So you go back and you erase what you did, and you do it again.

When you get to the end of something like that, you don't necessarily feel proud. You just feel tired. But you know you've earned your pay.

Q: What do writers and other editors look like, in copyeditors' eyes?
A: They look sloppy. Most of them look very sloppy. And sometimes so sloppy that I couldn't do as good a job—I couldn't do as much polishing, as much perfecting, as I really would have liked to do, because I was just too busy correcting stuff that was all garbled up. It makes you mad. Can't they do any better than that?

And then, over the years, it occurs to you, no, they can't. But the more the writer or the supervising editor can do to improve a piece, starting at the biggest level but on down into the smaller levels, the higher the level that everybody else—including the copyeditor—can work at.

If you don't have to be just hacking your way, with a machete, through the jungle, you can pay closer attention to where the flowers are, and whether the leaves are neat and tidy. You can really go a much longer way toward making that piece its best self.

Supervising editors, as well as copyeditors, are very grateful to writers who turn in clean, well-thought-out pieces that they don't have to struggle with.

If you are writing something, you think, *Well, there's a copyeditor to do that.* No, no. Think again. Try to get it the best you can, so you get the highest-level help out of the copyeditor.

I have seen that gratitude toward clean, well-thought-out pieces— writers who turn those things in—from every side of the desk. As the copyeditor, as the assigning editor, as the writer.

It is true that the most important thing is that the writer knows something that is going to be interesting to readers, that the readers will want to know—and that is why terrible writers who know interesting stuff continue to get work. But terrible writers who don't know anything very special don't get invited back. And wonderful writers who don't know anything very special sometimes do get invited back.

Q: How can writers and assigning editors get the most benefit from copyeditors and the least grief?

A: Well, by caring about details and upholding standards, and letting it show. One example of someone who did that, very charmingly. A long time ago, we had a humor piece by Roy Blount. And somewhere in it, he used the word "layup." I guess we were talking about basketball.

Well, in our dictionary or our style manual, it was hyphenated, and Roy really didn't like that. I remember getting a postcard from him, with just his signature and a little clipping from *The New York Times*, which used the word "layup" with no hyphen in it.

And we still hyphenated it, because that was our style. But it made me have a lot of respect for Roy, and the fact that he did care about the details of language.

I think now that if I were going to do that again, and since "lay-up" doesn't appear in *The Atlantic* all that often, I might look the other way, because his point was that it was funnier without a hyphen. And, you know, he's kind of right. It is funny, a layup.

A few years ago, he did something even more charming. In a piece of his, we had—he had written, "O tempora, o mores." You know, that Latin thing. And that fell between the cracks of fact-checking and copy-editing. I don't speak Latin. I figured the fact-checkers were going to check that. And they thought, *Well, Barbara knows all about words; we don't have to check that.*

So it came out, "O tempera"—T-E-M-P-E-R-A. And some indignant reader wrote in and said, "Well, that's an egg-based paint. I think you were talking about the word for 'time' in Latin." So, Letters to the Editor—over to you, Roy, to respond to that. And he said, "Oh, well, you're so right that we got the word wrong, but actually I was referring to fried Japanese food, and it should have been 'O tempura, o mores.'"

Thank you, Roy. That was nice.

So, to get the most out of copyeditors, if you can care about the stuff that they care about, good. And by the way, if you are a copyeditor and you work for someone who doesn't care about that stuff, now your job is to persuade those people that some, possibly many, of your readers do care, and that they never have to think about it again. Just leave it to you; it will all be taken care of.

The second way to work well with copyeditors is to try to have a human relationship with them. The way most organizations are set up, it won't be part of the workflow ever to talk to the copyeditor. And you may have to go a little bit out of your way to do that. But try to anyway.

I can think of a lot of pieces that could have been better, and better faster, if somebody had come to talk to me about them. And as it was, I often had to take my very best guess about what the writer would go for, without knowing anything about the writer as a person.

And all my thoughts about that piece were conveyed in little blue notes in the margin, with no chance for give and take. So if there was anything that I thought was pretty important and it just got overlooked in the course of talking with the writer, we would have to go around again at a later stage, and fight it out; where, if people had just talked to me a little bit more, I think it would have worked out better for all of us.

But try not to waste the copyeditor's time. And you can, if you are another editor at a magazine, waste a lot of a copyeditor's time, very unintentionally, by, say, rewriting or letting the writer rewrite whole, long paragraphs of a piece that has already been copyedited, when it turns out that the rewriting really is just adding a few words here and there.

Or maybe that particular complaint has to do with old-fashioned galleys, because your track-changes mode and the new ways of doing things can be unbelievably helpful.

But again here, so can talking with the copyeditor—not about specific pieces, but about ways of working that will be efficient for you both. The greatest good for the greatest number. I don't save myself ten minutes in order to waste an hour of your time.

And the fourth way to get along well with copyeditors is to recognize that they have an actual knowledge base and skill set that you probably don't have.

Where did that knowledge and skills come from? Reference books. Because there is no universal standard for things like spelling and capitalization; that's why there are different style books. The most widely used style books are AP and the *Chicago Manual*. There are zillions of others.

The Atlantic used to follow a style book called *Words Into Type*, and that was good, as far as it went. But the newest edition came out in 1974, and a lot has happened to the printed word since then—you know, like URLs. So over time, increasingly, we were more and more on our own. Today, if I had to choose, I think I would be in favor of *Chicago* for something as wide-ranging and literary as *The Atlantic*.

Dictionaries: The most widely used dictionary in publishing and in the whole country is *Merriam-Webster's Collegiate*—often called "Web Eleven," because it's in its eleventh edition. I think it is not a very good dictionary. My favorite is the *American Heritage*. But if Web Eleven is what just about everyone uses, that's a pretty good reason to use it, just because that's how people are used to seeing the words.

Style books and dictionaries include a little bit about these fine points of the language. But if you care about how to use particular words and how not to, what you really need is a usage manual. And if you wanted to build a copyeditor's reference shelf, here is what I would suggest, with the things I would suggest first, first.

The Careful Writer, by Theodore M. Bernstein, who for a good long time was in charge of style at *The New York Times*. And two other books, which are less well known, are *Miss Thistlebottom's Hobgoblins* and *Do's, Don'ts and Maybes of English Usage*.

All his stuff was intended for journalists, not for children who don't know anything about grammar and not for linguists and grammarians. It's intended for journalists. It's written in a good, clear style. He gets in his good explanations. And that book in particular, *The Careful Writer*, is still very widely respected.

Much more comprehensive and much more up to date is *Garner's Modern American Usage*, which was published in 2003, as opposed to 1965, which is when *The Careful Writer* came out.

But Garner is coming at language from a background in legal writing, not journalism, so more of the book than you might like is devoted to the proper use of things like "ex officio" and "ex cathedra." And a few—I mean it when I say "a few"—of Garner's opinions are eccentric, at least as they relate to normal practice in publishing. But the whole thing is an impressive work of scholarship, and it's the closest thing to a really comprehensible and up-to-date usage manual that we have.

Fowler's Modern English Usage is kind of the Beethoven's Ninth of the usage-manual world. Everybody admires it, but not everybody understands it. It took me years to understand parts of it, because Fowler's background was as a classics teacher in England in the '20s. So, quite reasonably, he thought that anybody who would read a usage manual understood a lot about grammar, which—among other things—is what you get out of learning Latin and Greek.

So he bandies about grammatical terms in a way that can be really quite intimidating. But you know, you can pick up knowledge of grammatical terms and what they mean as you go along. It is not really all that mysterious. And *Fowler's* also includes some very accessible—even lovable—essays about things like word choice, and when it is right to break the rules of grammar.

Please note that I am talking about the second edition of *Fowler's*. There was a third edition, sometime within the past ten years, *The New Fowler's*, by R. W. Burchfield. Maybe people in England like it, I don't know. But nobody uses it here. Enough said.

May I suggest that you buy your own reference books? Don't decide that there is no need to keep educating yourself, just because your employer won't pay for your books. Carpenters buy their own tools; so do most tradespeople.

The advantage to buying your own books is not only that you can get everything you think you need—and you can afford to; usage books, reference books, are available quite easily and inexpensively secondhand, online. But also, if you change jobs, you can take your books with you. And you don't have to start all over again, collecting them.

May I also suggest that anything that you can have put on your computer—like dictionaries—you do. I have, I think, seven dictionaries on my computer. Mostly, you can buy a CD-ROM along with the printed edition that adds five or ten dollars to the cost of the dictionary. Put it on the computer.

And having it on your hard drive is much more efficient than looking it up on the Web sites that those dictionaries may have. It's just a lot faster if you already have it on your computer. And both of those methods are a lot easier than heaving yourself up out of your chair and going and flipping through a book.

I also have access to the OED Online. And that's a lovely luxury, because it is much more often updated than the regular OED. But I mention that just to tell you that a lot of people really love the OED, but it is not practical as a first dictionary.

What it is really about is word histories. But it is not nearly as good as up-to-date American dictionaries about what words currently are in use and what they mean. So the OED is a fun reference, but not something that you particularly need in journalism.

Did you know that there is a frequently updated version of the *AP Stylebook* online? You can add your own rules to it. You could all share one, and people could add rules. That's a really cool thing. And one of the great things about it is that if any huge news event happens—let's say the country goes to war in Iraq—all of a sudden, place names that you have never heard of before, or prominent Iraqis, turn up in the *AP Stylebook*. So you don't have to be scrambling to research the right way to treat those things.

Just by the way, the second book I wrote, *Your Own Words*, goes on and on, probably in much too great detail, about the differences between dictionaries and differences between style books, the other kinds of reference books. So if you are interested in reference books, that is what the entire book is about. And it includes a big section about how to use things like LexisNexis and Google News; not just for the information in the stories, but to see how journalists today are using language.

And you can almost be your own dictionary maker now. You can get much more up-to-date reads on how respectable publications and respectable journalists are using the language than you ever could before electronic things were available.

So once again, count me in favor of the twenty-first century. Electronic resources are definitely the coming thing. But there is still an awful lot—unfortunately, an awful lot—that copyeditors need to know that can only be found in books.

Q: If copyediting is so wonderful, why aren't you doing it anymore? And what are you doing instead?

A: Well, I am not doing it anymore because being a copyeditor taught me how many people, besides professional writers, really care about the niceties of language, and how many people really wish they knew more about them.

Conversations at parties, telling people what I did at *The Atlantic*, would run either of two ways. People would say, "Oh, well, then I am afraid to talk to you." I guess that's kind of like being a psychiatrist at a party.

I also had an awful lot of conversations in which people would say, "Well, then, you must know the difference between 'that' and 'which.'" Or, "I hear there is something about 'compare to' and 'compare with' that I am supposed to know." And a lot of people get really excited: "Oh, you know something about that. Please tell me."

So I started writing the "Word Court" column, and that has been going on for eleven years. And I have been doing the newspaper version every week for two-and-a-half years. And I am just never going to run out of material. The questions keep coming, and the answers keep being interesting.

Something else that copyediting taught me was how to be a writer. You can't follow behind professional writers, including some of the really good ones, for twenty years and not pick up some techniques.

I don't actually know whether there is a better way of learning to write than getting in there, line by line, improving somebody else's stuff, and getting feedback from them on whether you have done what you hoped to do. And then, from readers—when you are working for a magazine, ask to be the person who answers readers' cranky questions about the language in your magazine, because you will learn a lot.

In my last few years of copyediting, I kept feeling, more and more often, *Man, I could write that better than whoever did*. So at that point, I began to feel it was time to move on.

So "Word Court" spun off the "Word Fugitives" column. And the "Word Fugitives" column spun off *Word Fugitives*, the book. And this is more fun than most of the other things that I've done.

7

How to Talk to the Art Director

Chris Dixon is the design director at *Vanity Fair*. At the time of this talk, he held the position of art director at *New York Magazine*. Prior to his tenure at *New York*, Dixon was art director of the multiaward-winning *Adbusters*, where he was responsible for the redesign and conceptual development of the magazine. He has also worked at *The New York Times Magazine* as editorial designer and has his own firm, Studio Plural, whose projects have included creating a new international design identity for the United Nations in publications and books from the HIV/AIDS division, and developing a new in-flight magazine for Lan Airlines in Chile. Chris Dixon spoke on February 17, 2010, with Victor Navasky acting as moderator.

MODERATOR: Let's start with the joke you made to me on our way to the lecture hall, about the art people and the editorial people being enemies. Why don't we begin with what happens when a writer turns in his piece?

CHRIS DIXON: Sure. The nature of a weekly magazine like *New York* is driven by the need for a fast turnover. We start planning based on the assigned length of the piece—3,000 words, 5,000 words, 8,000 words, what have you, and that's what it's been planned to. So the writer is supposed to write to that length. The editor is working with the writer during this process. And because it's a weekly, we have to put the magazine together as this is happening—as the writer is writing, a lot of times—so we have to design with this estimated word count. So we'll be told 4,000 words, and we are going to work—and we have the photography or the illustration that we've commissioned, and we do all our typography and we put the design for the story together.

Then a lot of times the story comes in, say, Wednesday night (we close the magazine Thursday night), and the writer will have had a breakthrough, and he's working at 4,500 words or 5,000 words rather than the 4,000 words he's been assigned. So that's where the enemy aspect comes in, because then the editor will come to us at 10 o'clock at night and say, "We've got to fit in another 700 words," and the result is that the photographs have to get smaller or things like the typography or the amount of white space have to be changed.

And then we have to go to the Editor-in-Chief, Adam Moss, and we all gather around and complain and make our cases. And he'll say, "Well, you can have 350 more words and make this photograph smaller." Then the photography director will scream because they spent $10,000 on this photo shoot and so you don't want to shrink the photographs any smaller then you have to. So that's the battle that goes on the last two days of finally closing a magazine. Of course, there are many positive things that happen before that.

M: I've had writers who tell me that they are intentionally late turning in their copy so people can't be mucking around with it and cut it. Now, these are writers who are old pros and who have the allegiance and respect of their editors.

CD: Right.

M: And this is what it's come to. Anyway, let me ask a question. Why is white space important? After all, it takes away our ability to put words in, which is what most people here want to do.

CD: I think overall, it's important for the pacing of the magazine. That's something we talk a lot about when we put together an issue. We build up a board of miniature versions of each layout (minis, we call them), and they're all up on the wall, and you can see how the issue is progressing page to page, story to story. We do things like build in more white space into one part of the magazine, in order to let it breathe—that's a term that we use, "Let's let this breathe." You want to give readers a harmonious feeling as they read a longer essay: build in white space, make the photographs bigger, don't have a cluttered layout.

But it depends on what part of the magazine you are in. For example, the "Strategist" section, which is the service part of the magazine, is designed to be really, really dense, so we actually don't pursue as much white space in that section. There we try to perfect the art of maximum content.

So we have multiple type sizes that are part of the design format, and they're consistent, so all the way down to a 7-point type size, which is very small, and 9-point, which is medium, and then 14-point, which is more for the quick read. So we build in all these different levels of type, and we make this section really dense, and then, say, when we get back into the "Culture" section at the end of the magazine, we'll open it up again and have more white space.

And so I think it works well with the pacing of the magazine, and it can give a certain story a luxurious or comfortable feeling while reading it. That will actually bring a certain tone to the story that you wouldn't have if it was packed in a lot denser.

M: How does an art director make basic decisions about a piece—whether it should have, for example, a photograph or an illustration? How do you decide that?

CD: The whole thing starts with a weekly meeting where we go through upcoming stories. We meet—that's myself and the photography director, Jody Quon, and then Adam Moss, the editor. And the three of us have that exact conversation—what does it look like, what's the visual strategy or the visual tone. Because you can go a thousand ways, you know, if it's a political story.

One example that we just did in one issue is the John Edwards story. We did an excerpt from the book *Game Change*, about the affair that John Edwards had while he was running for president. So there's a conversation about how we present this visually. Obviously we can't do photographs of scenes that happened because there were never photographers present at the time.

So we did something like a graphic novel, in which a graphic novelist or illustrator creates a sequential narrative throughout the piece and illustrates scenes that happened. The reader can experience the play-by-play of what happened, illustrated in this graphic-novel style. They're not static illustrations, they're multipaneled things. That's one strategy to illustrate a story.

Other things are more obvious. If you have a famous person or a famous politician, ideally you want to get access to photograph them so that you have an exclusive photograph—then it's our own portrait. It's done for *New York Magazine*. You can also get photographs by what's called pick-up, which means it's already run somewhere else or a photograph that's preexisting, and you just pay a fee and you run it, but it's not exclusive to your magazine. So if you're doing a story on a public figure, you call and get access and permission, and take a portrait of him.

M: You pose him and ask him to do strange things; do they lend themselves to that degrading ritual?

CD: If you're able to get some public figure to play along on a conceptual image, then you take advantage of that. A lot of times the reality is that the photographer will get 5 minutes or 3 minutes. If you're doing someone like Al Sharpton, they'll be in the middle of their busy day, and their people will say, "At 12:30, you get 5 minutes with him." So the photographer will come early, set up the backdrop, set up his lighting, getting ready. The person will come in and sit down. Then you shoot a bunch of pictures—you try to get the most interesting picture you can in that amount of time.

Sometimes someone really wants to do things like dress up or put on different outfits or put on makeup. And certainly the bigger the magazine, the more likely that is. *Vanity Fair* is the master. People want to be in *Vanity Fair*, and they will be working with Annie Leibowitz or another famous photographer, so they'll be happy to do things like get in a bathtub or dress up out in a field and those kind of things. So it all depends on the relationship.

If you photograph someone, you want to just see a portrait of them, you know, in real time; otherwise, for the more conceptual things, we find ways to illustrate, or we just do straight illustration, like caricature or things like that.

M: And should there be contact between an author and an illustrator in the ideal situation? And what is the norm? I've worked at magazines where they don't let the author near the illustrator. They don't let the author near the headline, even. It's just, you turn in your piece, you work until it's in shape, and then you're out of the picture. But what do you do, and what is the ideal relationship there?

CD: We don't have much contact with the actual writer of the piece. We deal with the editor of that piece, and the editors work on staff for our magazine, so we see them throughout the day. And they're in contact with the writer. We won't go to the author except when we need a certain amount of information for it. But we'll go to the editor. We'll have a meeting and we'll say, "What's this story about?" and he'll interpret what the writer's going to write because his job is to guide the writer through the process, as well. So we just deal straight with the editors.

M: What should writers and editors know about typography and fonts, or would you rather they know nothing and leave you to do what you know?

CD: Well, some magazines are more formatted than we are in how they present the longer feature stories in the middle of the magazine, with a set font size and the headline and subheadline strictly in newspaper style. We do a more expressive treatment of the headline inside, so it relates to the story. You can create some drama for the piece and have it work off the photograph. So we pay a lot of attention to typography. We chose a set family of typefaces for the magazine when we redesigned it, and we don't stray from that. We have a family of about five typefaces, and we rotate those for different things, depending on the use in the magazine. I think that gives the magazine part of its visual identity, and a consistency that the reader wants.

So we have five typefaces. We use them on the cover. And when we introduce a new one, it's a big deal and we go through a period of experimentation—you don't want to disrupt the feeling of the magazine. About a year and a half ago we started using a new typeface named Egyptian. It's actually a typeface that *New York Magazine* used in the '60s and '70s. It was one of their original typefaces.

So we introduced that, and it makes the designers happy because they have something new to work with. It's a different shape. It's got a different feeling that it brings to it.

M: Is it possible to articulate beyond the fact that it's new, so that gives you variety, that it's readable because it has certain characteristics? Beyond those obvious things, what are the principles on which one makes a type selection? It's hard to have this conversation without having the fonts in front of us.

CD: Well, I don't know how much everyone knows about typography, but there's a serif typeface, which is the thinner one with the serifs on the end. And those are used for the body text, and so that's the main stuff that you read, the smaller stuff. That's all set up just for pure readability and legibility.

But we also use that typeface in bigger sizes, and when it gets bigger it becomes more expressive. For example, if there's an article about a scandal or some sort of tabloid story, we'll use one of the sans-serif typefaces, one of the big, fat, thick, black ones, and we'll get a lot of size on those, and they'll give this sort of urgent feeling, and kind of shout the headline. On another story that's more of an essay, we'll do something smaller with a serif typeface, and that has more of a bookish kind of feel to it. It really does change the experience of the story.

Some editors we work with aren't as sensitive to it, not because of any fault of theirs, it's just the way they are. They'll just work on their stories and the words, and when they see the layout, they'll just say, "That's great." But the editor of the magazine, Adam Moss, is very savvy to design and visuals. So we'll present our designs to him, and part of the design will be how we interpret the headline and the size of it. And he'll see it, and he'll say, "No, no. This is all wrong. It's like it's shouting, and I want it to be really calm and feel like a beautiful reading experience." So then we'll adjust the design through the typography to have a different tone. He comes and looks at it and lets us know when he feels we're interpreting the story properly.

M: I remember once at *The Nation*, the great artist and caricaturist David Levine once did a great caricature for an article about the neo-Nazis in this country. It showed Uncle Sam with the Hitler moustache. It was a very striking image. The writer got very upset, and she said, "This is the opposite of what I was saying." And we ran it, on the theory that it wasn't the opposite of what she was saying, it was a way of drawing attention to what she was saying, and it worked no matter what you thought she was saying.

CD: Right.

M: But my question is, do you sometimes have writer reactions to the art direction that cause you problems? You have an editor in Adam Moss who understands art direction in a way that many editors don't. I wonder what you wish writers could understand about what your role is, and editors could understand about what your role is.

CD: One thing about *New York Magazine* is that a lot of our writers are on staff, so they actually have a section in the office where they have their cubicles, and they spend their days, or part of their days, there. So they're free to walk the halls and see what's going on. So if they're working on a cover story that week, they will wander down near my office, and I usually have the various covers we're working on outside my office. And they'll often stop and look. They might say they love it and move on, but other times they'll go to their editor and say something, and then they'll be told to come back to us.

M: Behind your back.

CD: Yeah, they go behind our back, and then an editor will come to us or to Adam and say that the writer of the piece does not like the cover. It's tough, because it's so close to them and they're writing it, and they have a certain perception of it. And they'll say that somehow it's wrong, or it's interpreting the piece wrong, or it just doesn't work for the cover that way.

M: I know you don't make any mistakes, Chris, but what are the mistakes that art directors make and what should a writer/editor do to intervene? Maybe you've already told us that—go behind your back and say, "Unmake that mistake." But what are the things that cause problems?

CD: I guess one thing would be not having a really solid understanding of the content that you're given, whatever the writer has written. And for our magazine, it's anything from long features to all the short pieces that are in the front section or the "Strategist," including charts and things like that that we have to visualize. The deeper your understanding of the content, the happier the writer will be with the outcome.

I think there's a general feeling that we don't read the pieces we're designing, that we'll get a headline, we'll get a summary, and then we'll just create whatever visual excitement we are feeling that day for our own satisfaction. A lot of times we'll have meetings about a story, and we will put together a presentation of how we're going to visualize it, and the editor will say, "Well, if you had read it, you would have known da, da, da." So they're assuming that we haven't read the piece and we don't understand. There's a sort of sense that we're not on the word side, so we wouldn't have read it.

So we try to approach it as journalists and read the stories and know the background and know exactly what goals of the piece are—at least, as much as we can on a weekly with intense time pressures. Once you get a core understanding of that, then you can visualize the story better.

M: You talked earlier about reviving a typeface that had been originally part of *New York*. How does a publication establish its visual identity, and how and why does it change, other than saying, "Well, we're tired of it. It's time for something new."

CD: We did a redesign of *New York Magazine* five years ago when basically a whole new staff came over with the editor, Adam Moss. In a lot of ways, a redesign will start with the editor's vision for the magazine. If there's a new editor at a magazine, they're going to want to put their stamp on it and give it a new approach, both editorially and visually. That process begins with long discussions with the editor about what their goal is and what they want for the look of it. And it's anything from, "I want it to be brash and tabloid and colorful and in-your-face," to "We want a very thoughtful, intelligent-looking, essay type of magazine." So there's a thousand ways to go. And to some degree the direction will be shaped by the publisher based on what's happening in the marketplace.

New York Magazine had gone through a journey in the '80s and '90s of different owners, and it became very commercial and very much about the best places to stay in the Hamptons and the best spas in New York—a really basic city magazine. But its roots were in really great journalism in the '60s and '70s. So I think Adam's goal was to take it back to that and get good writers and have more of an impact on the city with the journalism.

So the initial redesign was based on a lot of the elements of the original design from the '60s, which was sort of stripped down. And we do things like we just use black typography for the most part, which I think gives it more of a newspaper feel, and it has a certain reader experience to it as opposed to, say, fashion magazines or fitness magazines, which would use lots of bright colors and do things in a more casual way. So that was our goal, to land somewhere between a newspaper and the early *New York* magazines, which were black type, really stripped down, but with lots of use of scale and size in the typography. We wanted an overall feeling that it's not over-designed, but designed in a smart way for the reader.

M: How has the new technology affected the job of designing magazines? I'm not talking about Web site design; I want to ask you about that in a minute. But just in terms of being an art director, and in terms of creating the look of the magazine, how does technology help or complicate or facilitate what you do?

CD: Things just happen a lot faster now. We use the Adobe InDesign program to design the pages. But things like enabled FTP and PDF and all the technology that makes things travel faster and working with digital photography—it all makes the job a lot faster and easier. We do it all on the laptop.

But for the most part, we don't bring any technology onto the pages. It's just that we produce the magazine a lot faster thanks to the way we work with illustrators and photographers.

M: When we were coming down in the elevator, you asked me about the iPad and whether a lot of people here are paying attention to it. And I was saying it's not taught, but it's in the elevators and in the corridors, and we talk about it a little in class. And I'm curious whether you think that—how you think the Apple tablet and other new inventions will change the quality of magazines, and the big question: Wwill they cease to exist on paper or not?

CD: Paper will live. The conversation about magazines existing online has been the dominant conversation for the last five years, because magazines suddenly needed to have a Web site, and it had to be competitive, and they had to get everything on their Web site. But just in the last three months, there's this technology, the iPad or the tablet, where the visual richness of a magazine is to some degree preserved, and you can go through and the pages are presented as they are, pages with the layout and typography—there are just added elements, like the ability to click through multiple photographs with a story.

I saw a demonstration yesterday of *Wired* magazine on a tablet. They do a lot of infographics in their magazine, and the tablet version brought the infographics to life, and you could touch on it and see the result of this information. If it was oil reserves, for example, you could go through and look at it interactively.

So I think it's changed things somewhat—rather than the magazine designers thinking that they need to learn all these Web design skills and translate to that, now it's looking as if we can take what we already do and expand it by using motion and touch technology, but maintaining the same way of thinking, where you commission illustrations, photography, and those all run. By comparison, the Web strips down the content into really digestible things that the traditional role of the art director doesn't have a part in.

M: But will magazines exist on paper or won't they exist on paper five years down the road, in your impartial judgment?

CD: I think they will exist on paper.

M: Yes. Me too. Good. Right answer.

CD: I think advertisers like it, as well. They like having the place to put their ads.

M: I want to ask one last question. I think I have a good eye for carica-ture, but not a good eye for design. If you are an editor or writer and have no particular aesthetic pretensions, how do you develop a good eye? How do you as a "word person" become more sensitive to, en-gaged by, tuned in to, the aesthetic principles of design?

CD: I guess it would just be a matter of exposing yourself to magazines that are considered well designed and well produced: ones like *Vanity Fair* and *Wired* magazine and food magazines like *Bon Appetit*, maga-zines that take the content of recipes and visualize it in a big dra-matic way throughout their magazine. So I guess just exposing your-self and looking at those things and seeing how the experience changes for you when you read a magazine. Because the straight words that an editor or writer works with take on another life and form once they enter a magazine. That's how readers are accustomed to interacting with your words—surrounded by pictures or broken up into different digestible bites.

We find a lot of times that editors are excited about the process. And even if they don't engage with it actively, they are usually excited when they see the end result, because they could never imagine that their piece would end up being presented that way. And there's a bit of a competition among editors. You know, five or six of our key edi-tors do most of the pieces, so if one piece gets a great photo-essay or some really great funny illustrations that are going to bring attention to that piece, they're excited because their piece is being presented in a compelling way. And then other editors will say, "Where's my magic? Why didn't you bring mine to life in that way?" And we'll say, "We don't have time."

M: And I assume that same competition goes on in terms of who gets the cover and what the visual of the cover is going to be. Could you share with us what the considerations are? I think we understand the newsiness consideration, but what are the cultural considerations and the aesthetic considerations, and how do they express them-selves in a cover discussion?

CD: Well, generally the editor will pick a story that he feels is the cover. You know, next week the cover will be the John Edwards piece, or it's going to be a story on gifted children. So a piece is chosen that is seen as having viability as a cover. But what will sometimes happen is that either the piece will come in not as strong as we had hoped, or the news will change somehow and it won't feel as relevant, or the visual that we put together just does not work as a cover. But meanwhile, maybe visuals are developing for another feature inside that are actually working, and we'll move that onto the cover because it's determined to be successful.

So there is a flexibility through the week as we do the magazine about what's going to make the best cover. And a lot of times our editor will change the cover midweek if something happens in the news.

I think the most famous example was two years ago or a year ago, when the Eliot Spitzer scandal happened in New York and he was caught with the prostitute. And that news came out on a Tuesday morning, and we were in the middle of working on an issue about something else. But Adam Moss made a decision to just drop everything, and that was going to become the cover and the cover story. So we had to generate all-new artwork between Tuesday and Thursday to run on the cover so that it would come out Monday and be relevant to that news cycle.

M: Forgive me, I forget. Did you put him on the cover, or the call girl on the cover, or both of them on the cover?

CD: We worked with the artist Barbara Kruger. We had Spitzer on the cover smiling, and then we had the red box that said "Brain" and it was pointing to his groin region. That was the cover. And that was it. And we got lucky, because we were able to produce that in a couple days. And it did become somewhat iconic.

8

Three Weddings and a Funeral

Tina Brown is a journalist, magazine editor, columnist, and talk-show host. In 1973 she won the Catherine Pakenham Award for Most Promising Female Journalist in Britain. Following a career as an editor of *Tatler* magazine and *Vanity Fair*, she became in 1992 the editor of *The New Yorker*. She resigned in 1998 to launch Talk Miramax Books and *Talk* magazine. She was the host of *Topic [A] with Tina Brown* on CNBC and a columnist for *The Washington Post* and the *New York Sun*. She is the author of the best-selling book *The Diana Chronicles* and is now the editor-in-chief of *Newsweek* and The Daily Beast.

It is great to be here, and I am ready to share all the things that I've learned in this checkered career I've had. I've called my talk "Three Weddings and a Funeral."

I've been lucky enough to get four great editing opportunities in my life. And tonight I am very happy to accept this invitation to share those experiences with you, because I have learned something different, really, from each one of them. Although I would say the one that perhaps I've learned the most from was the one that didn't work—*Talk* magazine, which closed earlier this year [2002].

Talk folded after two and a half years of life, just when it had hit its stride. In the ad recession that deepened after the shock of 9/11, our investors were just too worried by the forecasts to keep going, which was understandable, but sad.

It had taken us a lot of agony at *Talk* before we started to succeed in that last year, and we folded at exactly the same moment when, 15 years previously, Condé Nast had seriously contemplated folding another magazine that I was editing at the time, *Vanity Fair*—which at that point had a much lower circulation than *Talk*, of 450,000, and about 35 ad pages.

In the case of *Vanity Fair*, we were able, I'm happy to say, to persuade Si Newhouse to give us another year of life. And we did take off and reached 1.1 million circulation and profit. So of course, he has no regrets today.

But what I learned from the *Talk* magazine flameout was twofold. First, the dynamics of a launch really have to be examined. No amount of experience and dedication can spare one the essential component of process. At the eureka moment of conception, it is very easy to overlook the fact that everything you're doing is going to change, that what you are to be engaged in is dynamic, a collision of variables, especially if you are trying to do something new.

Whether it is a magazine or a TV show or a comedy act or a play or a book publishing house or a movie company, certain kinds of ambitious creative ventures have to be forged in live experiment—they must change course, try on identities, and even go up a blind alley or two before they find any kind of inner coherence.

I think almost the first thing they learn at West Point is that no battle plan survives contact with the enemy. Given what I call the "double V," the velocity of the variables, the venture either has to have enough time and money to fail for a time, or more realistically—because, frankly, who has that luxury?—perhaps it's better to skip an ambitious launch and perfect the trial-and-error process under cover by starting out of town or building frequency very slowly. Elizabeth Hardwick once said, "Magazines are like mushrooms. They should grow in the dark."

Talk, I know with 20/20 hindsight, perhaps would have been better served by a batch of test issues out of New York. But then again, my partner, Ron Galotti, and I were extremely high-profile people. And we were trying something out of the ordinary: not just a magazine, but a media company that would be linked by synergies. And the magazine itself would be a very different product as well.

What I wanted to do was a more European kind of magazine that would fuse aspects of the newsmagazine culture with aspects of the glossy-magazine culture—in a form and size a little out of the ordinary. We needed more time to prepare people for it and refine it. Instead, *Talk* did all its rehearsal in the baleful glare of maximum exposure, and that was actually very destructive to the commercial and creative process.

The second thing I learned was that personal heroics on the part of a staff can't defeat overwhelming market forces. An awful lot of cold-eyed analysis has to be done to determine how much a new idea is just the obsession of its creator. I have always worked more out of passion than pragmatism myself, and I think I'd started to believe that passion could defeat any odds. But it can't.

The chemistry and commitment of your backers, the response of your newly alert competitors, the resources made available to them to fight back, the condition of the economy, and the luck—there is no other word for it—of finding exactly the right people to work with you at the right moment: all these elements have to be in total alignment to achieve success. Now, I don't mean to suggest that market analysis alone can guarantee success or predict failure, and I'll come back to that when I talk about *Vanity Fair*.

I got my first editing chance at the *Tatler* in London when I was 25. The *Tatler* was an almost defunct society monthly with a circulation of 10,000, which was acquired for very little money by an Australian real-estate guy who thought he would try his hand at publishing. He hired me, I think, after everybody else had turned him down. At the time I was this kind of young Turk reporter at *The Sunday Times* and the *New Statesman*.

I had never edited anything before, and all my friends thought that a society magazine was incredibly uncool, especially one that seemed to be in some kind of terminal coma. The *Tatler* had a tiny budget and no more than twelve employees, including me. But I was excited by the idea of putting together a motley brand of editorial free spirits, if I could find them. And I did, on the fringes of journalism. I think what they had in common besides talent was they didn't fit in anywhere else. The *Tatler*'s young editors seemed to thrive on a very nonhierarchical kind of shop, and I think small magazines are a very good cover for sort-of renegades who are prepared to work all night.

When I started at the *Tatler*, I did something that I subsequently did at *Vanity Fair* and at *The New Yorker*—I think of it now as trying to recapture the DNA of a publication. In *Tatler*'s case, I went all the way back as far as the eighteenth century, the very first issues of the first magazine, and found them animated by the writing of the satirist Jonathan Swift, who wrote *Gulliver's Travels*, and the political essayists Joseph Addison and Richard Steele. They had contributed to the magazine when it was a sharp-tongued literary pamphlet, fashionable with the coffeehouse culture of Georgian England.

After this era, *Tatler* fell apart for a few hundred years, until the early twentieth century, when it resurfaced as a society picture weekly full of snaps of debutantes sipping warm sherry at country-house parties in Gloucestershire—think *Gosford Park*. It was incredibly lightweight, but delightful, and there was a buoyancy about the *Tatler* of the '20s that exuded the social confidence of that time.

I wanted all of this feeling in the new version that we were planning to put out. Looking back at what we did at the *Tatler* in the early '80s, I can see how we stumbled around a bit until, almost unconsciously, we forged a magazine that reflected a fusion of *Tatler*'s past and present. Our new writers were irreverent and edgy with a literary tone. I identified with my snotty friends like the young Martin Amis, Christopher Hitchens, and Julian Barnes, or the twenty-two-year-old Cambridge graduate that we hired, Nick Coleridge, who is now Managing Director of the British Condé Nast.

At *Tatler*, we managed to break news and bite the hand that read us. And we did it all with a lot of attitude. I learned early on that if you don't have a budget, you must have a point of view.

All of this, though, would not have been commercially successful if the timing and the marketplace had been out of sync. I now see that *Tatler* was reborn at exactly the right moment, when Mrs. Thatcher's

Tory government was bringing a second lease on life to the fraying, braying upper-middle classes. We lucked into what every magazine must have—relevance.

When Prince Charles announced his engagement to Diana Spencer—and the Lady Di saga was to the *Tatler* what O. J. was to CNN—circulation grew from 10,000 to 40,000. And our trusty real-estate guy, of course, ran out of money just at the critical juncture and sold the magazine to Condé Nast.

We were very small fry to Condé Nast when the British arm of the company bought us. The head office in New York was already preoccupied with their own DNA experiment. They had decided to relaunch their old title that had been retired for the previous forty-odd years, *Vanity Fair*. The company was in the midst of a brilliant and expensive ad campaign to precede it. So brilliant that it was lethal.

The raising of expectations is a surefire way to get any new business trashed. But it is a real conundrum, unfortunately, if the goal is to launch a big commercial general-interest magazine, as we found later. The new *Vanity Fair*, like *Talk*, had to go after the big-time glossy fashion, beauty, and automobile categories of advertising.

And although it is risky to raise expectations, it is also pretty difficult to sell 100 pages of color advertising at $35,000 if you say, "We're going to start rather slowly and we're going to stumble around and in about six months we're going to be okay." I mean, the fact is, you have to come out gunning on all sides.

With *Vanity Fair* the drum rolls definitely did sell Madison Avenue, and it broke all the ad records when it launched in 1983. But the hype was also very, very destructive, and ten months in, the ads had vanished and Condé Nast was looking for a third editor, amid expectations of closure.

From across the Atlantic, perhaps, in a moment of desperation, Mr. Newhouse reached out to me and offered me the hot seat. It took me at least twenty minutes to accept. I'd always dreamed of moving to New York, and in the words of E. B. White, "I was willing to be lucky."

Arriving from London as the new editor-in-chief in January 1984 in a freezing New York winter was a scary business. I did have one advantage, though, that I didn't have at *Talk*: there was nowhere to go but up.

Vanity Fair was down to 12 advertising pages and a circulation of 250,000. It did also mean that I inherited a lot of other horrible problems. A demoralized staff, and coming straight from London, I just didn't have the same Rolodex of writers and photographers that I'd had at the *Tatler*. The advertising community was completely turned off, and also, there was something I used to call the New York jab, where I would go out to lunch and people would stab their index fingers in my chest and say, "When's your magazine going to fold?"

The conventional wisdom at the time was that there was no market niche for a general-interest magazine. If I heard it once, I heard it a hundred times, and read it all the time in the trade press—niche magazines were in, general magazines out. What on earth had Si Newhouse been thinking about?

Well, actually, he'd been thinking pretty well, it was just that the execution, so far, hadn't been right. The marketplace and the timing were right. We just had to find the right key for the lock, and there was no one to blame but ourselves if we fumbled. Condé Nast gave us every freedom, every resource, including Alexander Liberman, the company's great editorial director, who taught me an enormous amount about the glossy magazine's need for expansiveness.

As with the *Tatler*, *Vanity Fair* was relaunched into the beginning of a new churn of the social waters: the Reagan era, with the Wall Street boom and all the new personalities that had risen along with it. There was no magazine out there at the time that was exploiting the social atmosphere of the burgeoning celebrity power and the postmodern media culture.

More important, as with the *Tatler*, the opportunity for new magazine entry was lying there unseen by the media pundits. I looked back at *Vanity Fair* of the '20s to see why that legend seemed to still live on. The pages still danced. I saw how artfully Frank Crowninshield, the editor at that time, combined the seduction of visual glamour with the edge of cultural and social commentary. There was the ravishing photography of Edward Steichen and the lively astuteness of writers like Clare Booth Luce, Robert Benchley, Alexander Woolcott, and Anita Loos.

But, exciting as it was, the old *Vanity Fair* seemed far too flip for a magazine of 1984. What had intervened between then and now had been the great Harold Hayes's narrative journalism in the heyday of *Esquire*, Jann Wenner's *Rolling Stone*, Clay Felker's *New York*. The reincarnated *Vanity Fair* needed, I thought, to recapture the stylishness and visual excitement of that Crowninshield era with this later strand of relevance and substantial journalism.

We needed to find a roster of contributors for our new mix, who would forge the magazine a clear, new identity, but most of the good ones were wary about signing on because they felt the ship was a bit like the *Titanic* at this point.

To get the ball rolling, I was going to have to take a chance on somebody perhaps less well known. I think maybe Frank Crowninshield's ghost smiled at me, because one evening in my first panicky weeks, I went to dinner with a star writer of *New York Magazine*, Marie Brenner, whom I had met in my *Tatler* days, and was hoping that I might be able to woo her to join us, which eventually I did, I'm glad to say.

She sat me next to a movie producer friend who was down on his luck and who was also trying to deal with a family tragedy. His daughter had been murdered and he was going out to L.A. to attend the trial of the killer. He and I bonded as the evening wore on, and I kept wondering if he could write well enough to attempt an article about what had happened to him. It has been my experience that nonprofessional writers are less scared of writing a letter or keeping a diary. In that form, they don't have a problem being themselves. I think that e-mail has also been able to liberate voices in the same way, which is one of the reasons Web magazines have found so many interesting new talents. So I didn't invite my dinner companion to write a piece; I suggested instead that he keep a diary.

Well, Dominick Dunne turned out to have one of the most important things that a writer can have: an authentic voice. He became our first contract writer, and it was his personal style of reporting on society, Hollywood, and crime that helped give the magazine some early definition.

What *didn't* define the magazine was some of our early covers, which were pretty disastrous. We tried idea covers, but they never seemed to come out right. One real bomb, I recall, was a Thanksgiving cover of Brooke Shields with a turkey on her head. God knows what we thought we were doing. But the press kept trashing us and advertisers remained unconvinced and news of our demise was pretty much a weekly occurrence.

In May 1985, I was in San Francisco speaking at an advertiser's function when the call came to say the next issue would be the last. I flew back to lobby everybody in the company (and certainly the publisher, Doug Johnston), promising that we had a lot of good things in the works and had just hit our stride.

To Si Newhouse's credit, I must say, he gave us one more year, and we did find our stride, with covers from the great celebrity photographers Annie Leibovitz and Helmut Newton and Herb Ritts. And in the next six months that followed, things finally began to fall into place.

Harry Benson produced the news-making cover of the Reagans kissing, and that was picked up all over the world. Dominick Dunne filed a brilliant, much-quoted story about the Claus von Bülow case, which ran with memorable, much-syndicated portraits of him in black leather by Helmut Newton. And actually, I was very happy to be denounced when I wrote a story breaking the news of the estrangement of Charles and Diana.

Advertising now grew as fast as the circulation did, and we were number one on *Adweek*'s "Hot List" two years in a row. We grew from 350,000 to 500,000 and then 900,000, when in 1991 Annie's cover shot of a naked Demi Moore pregnant shot the circulation past the million mark. It has stayed up there ever since. And in our seventh year we were profitable at last, with issues of up to 250 pages and revenue that grew steadily.

What had I learned? That to maintain momentum, you must rejoice in risk. Demi Moore was one kind of a risk, but another was infiltrating unfrothy foreign affairs, politics, and literary content among all the flash and the dash of the magazine.

William Styron's long essay on his depression, which we persuaded him to write after he had spoken at a fundraiser for suicide survivors, took us, I think, to a new literary level. Especially when it developed into a best-seller that used our title, "Darkness Visible."

Si Newhouse then gave me another really great opportunity in 1992. He invited me to be the fourth editor of *The New Yorker*. This time I had to learn something that went really against the grain for me: how to manage a venerable institution that was so sensitive to the smallest, smallest little change that every new decision had a thousand ramifications and offshoots.

My predecessor, Robert Gottlieb, had been deeply sensitive about this, almost to the point where he had seen his role as that of a curator. But *The New Yorker* was facing some very serious economic problems. The advertisers that had been the envy of Condé Nast when they launched *Vanity Fair* in '83 had drained away, concerned about the steadily aging readership. Legendary *New Yorker* talents toiled behind the closed doors of their offices, but some hadn't turned in a piece for as long as five years or even twenty years, as in the case of the great Joseph Mitchell.

New talent rarely penetrated. Sometimes it seemed that it was writers, writers everywhere, but not a drop to drink in the sense that every time you asked anybody to do a piece they would say, "Great idea, but I'm just writing this great long article for six months' time on the seascape," or something. You could never get anybody to actually write something for the issue. So I had to find new people.

It seemed to me that the talent that was there was often left to write at inordinate length, regardless of the intrinsic interest of the subject matter. I have been very happy to give writers length when I felt that it was earned; in fact, I gave Mark Danner a whole issue of the magazine to write about the massacre at El Mozote. But I didn't agree with length just for length's sake.

The New Yorker had to regain, I felt, relevance, the place that it had once enjoyed in the cultural conversation when it led opinion in its heyday. It had to exploit being weekly without falling into the trap of responding in a pedestrian way to headlines, and it needed to find and nurture a new generation of writers who could continue the great literary pedigree of John McPhee and Roger Angell and John Updike and many, many more.

Of course, the *New Yorker* staff in place didn't see my arrival in those terms at all. They looked at Demi Moore's pregnant stomach on the front of *Vanity Fair* and thought, *The anti-Christ has arrived.* I mean, there was a lot of a suspicion, hostility, and negative comments. And there was a contentious meeting, I remember, with cartoonists who were convinced there was a plot to supplant them with Annie Leibovitz. But of course, I had no plans to do that; in fact, I gave them their own annual special cartoon issue to celebrate at a greater spot size and space.

With the writers, however—it was not the writers you might think of as the quote, old guard, the real old-timers like Lillian Ross and Harold Brodkey, Edith Oliver, Roger Angell, who were actually antagonistic to what we were doing. They remembered the days when the magazine had a much faster tempo, and they had missed the response that pieces used to get before the heartbeat slowed down. And they were actually very open to me.

The writers, I think, who were the noisy antagonists to our new broom were those who came in the last era of William Shawn, when they sensed the door was about to close on them and on the club that defined them. They were always quoted in the papers, but in fact, they were pretty marginal to the ongoing process of the magazine.

It was, in fact, the octogenarian staffer Brendan Gill who encouraged me all the way. "They forget," he told me, "that *The New Yorker* was never a static magazine. There have been many *New Yorker*s: early Harold Ross and late Harold Ross and early William Shawn and late William Shawn." And Harold Brodkey, who was a writer I adored, also admonished me. He said, "Don't be strangled by fake ivy."

So again I went to the library, to the very first issues of the '20s and '30s to see what Harold Ross had had in mind when he launched *The New Yorker* in 1925. It was, as Brendan Gill had told me, incredibly different from *The New Yorker* of later years, and I felt an instant affinity with it. The Ross magazine was fast-paced, responsive, graphically much more alive, with shorter articles and a mix of very short and long pieces that to me had a much more reader-friendly rhythm. The covers by Peter Arno and Charles Addams were strong and mischievous and colorful, and the pieces in "The Talk of the Town" were actually as short as 250 words, which I was never able to achieve in my era. The Ross *New Yorker* gave off a kind of sophisticated, lively feeling that felt very much in touch with the spirit of the times.

I wanted to develop that early Ross DNA, but also to keep and nurture the essential strand of high-quality writing and reporting in the celebrated years of Shawn. To do that, I had to identify those staff writers who could adjust and excel in the new era and those who were just frankly burned out. There were also a number who just wanted a change of direction, like the incredibly talented Adam Gopnik, who was the art critic but was obviously bored. I sent him to Paris, and he wrote the essays that have become his book, *Paris to the Moon*.

So, while trying to nurture and reassure the best of the writers that we had, we also added this enormous new layer of talent. In six years, 79 writers and editors left, and 48 new writers and editors joined. It was a source of pride to me that we kept the loyalty of the best. I mean, I really would have hated to lose Roger Angell or John Updike, or Janet Malcolm or Brendan Gill, Mark Singer, Whitney Balliett, Oliver Sacks, Arlene Croce, or the brilliant nonfiction editor John Bennet.

But to mix old and new blood, we needed editors and managers of considerable sophistication and maturity if it all wasn't going to be just a huge mess. From *Vanity Fair* I took my key executive, Pam McCarthy, who really helped to keep the ship steady, and from *The New Republic* I took Hendrik Hertzberg, who had the advantage, actually, of having worked at *The New Yorker* many years before, so he knew where all the bodies were buried.

It took me another two years to complete the team with Dorothy Wickenden and Henry Finder and Jeffrey Frank and Bill Buford, who joined us from *Granta*. With these editors in place, I knew that both old and new writers would be served by some of the most talented executives that I had known. And we needed them to work with the talent that now came on board.

One of my first hires, actually, was David Remnick from *The Washington Post*, who became my successor, I'm very happy to say. He had been writing brilliantly from Moscow and he joined in my first year. Others who came over the next few years were Henry Louis Gates from

Harvard's African American studies department; John Lahr; Malcolm Gladwell from *The Washington Post*, who developed one of his pieces into the best-selling book *The Tipping Point*; intrepid investigative journalists like James Stewart, Seymour Hersh, Jane Mayer. And then there were people like Simon Schama who were risks that we took, in the sense that Simon was a historian. We gave him the opportunity to become the art critic and he was a great success immediately, as was Anthony Lane, the film critic from London.

And then there was a Dominick Dunne-style risk that we took on a young assistant U.S. attorney in Brooklyn called Jeffrey Toobin. He came into his own with the O. J. trial, and he is now very important to the magazine. He is also the legal affairs correspondent for CNN.

I think perhaps the most conceptual of the risks that we took was in the attitude to covers and photography. We wanted to keep the urbanity of the best of the traditional illustrations, but we also wanted to suggest some of that fizz going on inside the magazine. And this was risky, certainly risky among worshipers of the fake ivy image that Brodkey had warned me about.

We commissioned covers from the master of creative anarchy, Art Spiegelman, who was the controversial cartoonist and author of *Maus*. And we brought on board Ed Sorel, a wonderfully witty illustrator, who I think should have been at *The New Yorker* long before, and hired a new cover director, Françoise Mouly, who was actually married to Art Spiegelman. And she brought in a raft of new illustrators who are now beautifully settled in, I think, as the *New Yorker* new generation.

And of course, we also brought in Richard Avedon. And we opened the windows and allowed photography in for the first time in a meaningful way.

It took a couple of years before *The New Yorker* began to gel as a coherent entity, and until the old and new cultures melded. The new readers were younger, but we also had the highest renewal rate in the business. What was much harder to achieve was convincing the ad community that the magazine had a new relevance. It was an uphill battle at *The New Yorker*.

Which brings me to *Talk*, a magazine I am just as proud of as all the others, if only because getting it right was such a challenge, and just when we had it, we lost it, which was bittersweet, I will admit.

But I learned that there is a whole world of difference between a startup and taking over an existing title. With a startup, all the time that needs to go to the creative process goes instead to the building of financial and operating infrastructures. My partner, Ron Galotti, who was the publisher of *Vogue*, joined forces with Miramax and Hearst and me to start not just a magazine, but a media company.

And the idea was a new one. Talk Media, as we called it, would comprise the magazine and an ancillary book company, both of which would look for the opportunity to also acquire movie rights for Miramax. Magazine and book company launched at the same time; we had to find staff for both of them at once and figure out how our synergies were going to relate to each other and work operationally.

The book company already existed as the skeleton, one-person operation Hyperion. Miramax had successfully published Quentin Tarrantino's screenplay of *Pulp Fiction* and agreed with Hyperion to distribute it.

Ron Galotti and I were able to start the book company under the radar, and as a result it grew in stealth and has been very successful. It's been a great success, actually, with five best-sellers in its first two years of life. And we also acquired Simon Schama, Martin Amis, and Michael Chabon as authors. So the house actually gained a lot of prestige as well as commercial success very quickly.

The magazine, however, was much harder to get right under the competitive pressures of that marketplace. And let's face it, we were the favorite blood sport of the press pack—400 media columns were written about us in our first two years of life, which has got to be a record. I warned the staff that it would be bad, but actually it was kind of a Hell's Angels initiation ceremony. And by the end of it we felt we had just fought more wars than Kabul. And it was extremely destructive to the process.

So, amid all the rotten tomatoes that were hurled our way, what in fact were we trying to do at *Talk*? Well, our original concept was a magazine with several strands, a European mix of a journalistic magazine like the successful German magazine *Stern*, combined with deeply personal reporting and as much unmediated reporting as we could find.

My hope was that we could tap into new voices from the alternative press and small magazines and the Web. And we actually did that successfully with writers like Tucker Carlson, Eddie Dean, Andrew Goldman, and Sam Sifton. Some of these voices found expression in diaries and oral biographies, of which I think the best received were the one we did on Clinton's White House by Richard Reeves, and the one on Marc Rich, and all the pieces of a highly autobiographical nature that we ran by writers like Tom Stoppard and Adam Bellow and Mimi Swartz and David Brock.

We wanted celebrity and fashion to be a much smaller part of *Talk* than of *Vanity Fair*. And then covers were the challenge. We sought covers that had multiple images, to escape from the tyranny of the celebrity chasing we had had to do at *Vanity Fair*.

And we printed the magazine on a newsy paper stock with saddle stitching, giving it a roll-up sort of portable feeling that we felt was a real point of difference. And there was a difference, all right. Advertisers hated it, and I mean hated it. They hated it so much that a year in we had to admit defeat and change format and go to glossy paper. That made them all want to advertise, and we felt they finally recognized what we were doing.

Stubbornly, I still love what the first issues of *Talk* tried to be and I feel, particularly in the wake of 9/11, that we were right to want to escape the connotations of a glossy magazine. I am just sorry that we didn't get the art direction and the packaging right enough or stick with it long enough before we yielded to the commercial pressures to change it. And I am sorry not least because the informality of feeling dictated by the format made it necessary to entirely reconceive the magazine on the run and dodge the bullets all along the way.

Well, that gave us a nine-month identity crisis that lasted through our second year, when the editorial musical chairs just kept changing. And they finally ceased when we gathered a brilliant young team together like we did at the *Tatler*, from all over the place—small magazines, fringe magazines. They were really an amazing group of people, and they finally settled in and bonded. They may have actually been among the most spirited and original staff that I have ever worked with, because in a sense, they found us.

Being willing to be a part of such a beleaguered and fast-moving venture as *Talk* attracted the most adventurous, brave, and crazy of the editors around town. But in our last eight months of life, with a new art director who reinvented our format on the slick paper—and new editorial director in the gifted Maer Roshan—we were actually putting out a first-class magazine with a much more reader-friendly front of book and a newsier feature content. And it did find an appreciative young audience.

There was great esprit de corps, and circulation and advertising really did very well in that last half of the year. We were 17 percent up in circulation, to 650,000, and 7 percent up in advertising at a time when most other magazines were already feeling, and reeling from, the bite of recession. But 9/11 did change our business forecast entirely. Our partners were going to have to take a really big financial hit to ride it out, and they didn't feel they could do that, especially in the light of how it was affecting their other businesses. Our book publishing company, Talk Miramax Books, however, does survive, and it prospers.

I still feel just as strongly that the basic synergistic idea for our company was very, very sound. The excitement generated by the magazine's culture and the constant flow of authors and submissions and shared editorial sensibilities were enormously stimulating for the book company. My guess is that as a magazine we were roadkill, but I am sure that we pioneered something valid and someone else will make a more endearing success of the tryout of magazine, book, and film. I think all who worked and cared at *Talk* know that we did share something unique, incredibly exciting and unforgettable, as every one of my very different magazine experiences has been.

> Seven years later, Tina Brown returned to speak to the Columbia audience, but in a different role and a different time.

We are in the middle of what I think of as a kind of media industrial revolution. The old structures are all crumbling around us, Aad new structures are going to have to be invented to preserve great journalism.

We know that to not have the kind of journalism that most of us care about means that we're going to be a very, very ignorant society and put our whole democracy in peril. We need real information, truthful information and inquiry and investigation and answers, or we will be plunged into chaos. I myself have moved out of the old world of print into the new world of online. And if you'd asked me a year ago, Would I really not miss the world of print?, I have to say that I couldn't believe that I would be as happy and fulfilled and as excited as I am by working on this new online venture that I've christened The Daily Beast.

I love narrative journalism, which those magazines I formerly worked at—*Vanity Fair*, *The New Yorker*, and *Talk*—allowed me to do. But there were also quite a lot of things that I couldn't do in those magazines. I found it unbearable, really, and very inhibiting, when I had to deal with the length of deadline that a monthly requires. Not just because it takes so long just to go to press, but because there is also that long wait between the delivery of the magazine and the day it hits the newsstand.

There's this whole agonizing week where you've got your magazine in the office and you're looking at it, but nobody else has it yet. And in that week, in today's insane media climate, everybody picks at that product and tears it apart and the news goes all over the place, so by the time you come out, some TV show has done the story, or some radio show has broken or stolen bits of it. And there's nothing left by the time the magazine comes out. You just have a big load of cold potatoes. And that just made me crazy, it was really very hard to bear.

So monthly journalism now has to really reinvent itself into being more conceptual and long-term, so that it really does set an agenda and create its own sort of niche. Because it really can't respond to the news at all. It's just too late.

So I was terribly excited last year when I was asked to take over—to invent, if you like—a new news Web site. My partner, Barry Diller, who has been an entertainment mogul and now has IAC interactive company, came to me and asked if I would like to start a news site with him that acted as a kind of sensibility guide through the news.

His feeling was that we're all completely overwhelmed with information. And what we really want is a smart friend to basically tell us what to read every morning, a friend who has a great eye for what the story is. What appealed to me about that was that in a sense, it's what I've always done as a magazine editor. After all, any magazine, whether it's monthly or weekly, is a menu of stories. You have to make a choice. And it's all about the editor's choosing, all about the sensibility, the eye, the sense of what's important, and the sense of priority.

I was attracted to the idea of creating a Web site that would offer an alternative front page every morning. And the great thing about being able to aggregate stories, as well as to produce your own original ones, is that it enables you to treat the Internet as an incredible banquet of news and stories, a feast you can choose from every morning.

So we have one editor and two interns who get up every morning about quarter to five, and they just read everything that they can get their eyes on. Quirky stuff, interesting stuff, mainstream stuff— whatever stuff. I chose them because I like the way they think.

And every day we do ten stories that we call the "Cheat Sheet," which is a cull of the stories that we think are the most interesting. And they then present them to the reader with a lot of opinion and attitude in the way they write them up. Because they provide a little 150-word "cheat," as we call it, which is a distillation of the story. But it's done with a lot of intelligence and attitude, and that provides the voice of the site.

Because any Web site needs a distinctive identity from the beginning. It's all about creating an atmosphere, creating a feeling of community with a certain kind of reader. And that's done with voice. That's something I've always spent a lot of time on in the magazines that I've edited. At *Vanity Fair* and *The New Yorker*, I probably spent most of my time as the magazine went to press writing the headlines, the decks, the blurbs that introduced the stories, the contents page, the captions, the pull quotes.

I think these are the most vital aspects for creating a voice in a magazine, because you have to tell people why something is interesting. They're busy, they don't really want to read anything, so you have to find a way immediately to ask them a question, prod them, interest them, amuse them, and provoke them to start reading that story.

It's enormous fun to do, and I think probably the most fun part of editing. I don't know how many of you spend your time doing it, but it's the real fun part of a magazine. And what I found online is that the most important thing any Web site can do is to give a sense of atmosphere, a taste as soon as people open it. So the "Cheat Sheet" about those ten stories, our alternative front page, is the core of the site.

When I began it I thought, *Well, I'm really going to miss doing narrative journalism.* And I do miss narrative journalism, I have to say. It's the one thing that doesn't really work that well online, because it's too long to engage readers. But what I do love is finding exactly the right writer for a subject. There is no greater resource for an editor than knowing exactly which writer is out there for any story you want to assign. And doing a Web site, I found it's been absolutely fantastic to know so many writers and to have spent so much time with them over the years, so that I really know what turns them on and what they can do.

And you also need to know their weaknesses, what you shouldn't let them do. There are many writers who love to do certain stories and aren't any good at them. And you have to kind of gently nurture them away from those stories. I used to spend a lot of time at *The New Yorker* with writers who would come in with something they wanted to do, and often I knew it was just what they shouldn't be doing. But this was this fatal attraction they had to certain kinds of stories, their comfort zone, which made them really boring and predictable.

What I would try to do is to really talk to them and hear what their passions actually were, because their passions weren't necessarily what they'd been writing about all those years. And so I did a lot of changing of people's patches. What I'm finding online is a great opportunity to act like a newspaper—to be fast-paced—but also to bring a voice to it, to bring an intelligence, and to bring a kind of counterintuition to the news. And we allow people who have got great opinions just to come in and voice them.

So I feel that the Web is providing a wonderful forum for voices to come and put ideas out into the national conversation, and have some impact. And it's exciting, and that's what we're focusing on at The Daily Beast, which is very exciting for us indeed.

9

The Simpler the Idea, the Better

Peter W. Kaplan is Editorial Director of Fairchild Fashion Group. At the time of this lecture, he was editor of the *New York Observer*, a position he held for fifteen years. He has also worked as creative director of *Condé Nast Traveler*; as a reporter at *The New York Times* and *The Washington Post*; as an editor at *New Times* magazine, *Esquire*, and *Manhattan inc.*; and as executive producer of Charlie Rose's program on PBS. This lecture was delivered Febuary 1, 2007.

How did I get into this game? When I was a kid, my dad used to bring *Esquire* home once a month. He'd unclick the briefcase and there was this big magazine with these covers, what I now recognize as George Lois covers, with big pictures and witty lines: there was Richard Nixon being made up by an army of makeup men, there was Hubert Humphrey as a marionette on Lyndon Johnson's lap. There was Svetlana Stalin with her father's moustache, and of course, there was William Calley surrounded by smiling Vietnamese children.

What kind of magazine was this? Inside there were pieces, long pieces by Gay Talese and Tom Wolfe and Gore Vidal. Sometimes the writers seemed to be the stars. In fact, the biggest stars in the whole *Esquire* universe seemed to be John F. Kennedy, Norman Mailer, and Ernest Hemingway.

Around the same time—I was a sophomore in high school—I saw a piece in *The New York Times Magazine* by Richard Reeves called "This Is the Battle of the Titans?" It was written in a way that I'd never seen anyone work in *The New York Times* before—first person, witty, and edgy. Almost every story seemed like it was fastball.

Somehow I knew what I wanted to do for a living.

I got into journalism right up here, at Columbia, when I was sixteen years old. I was here for a conference of high school newspaper editors, and Reeves spoke. It was love at first sight. He was everything I thought a newspaperman should be: funny, wry, and he sounded like Robert Mitchum. I chased him and caught up with him at the subway. "Mr. Reeves," I asked him, "do you need an assistant?" He laughed. But six years later I wrote him and reminded him that he had said yes, and he hired me to work on a book on the 1976 Democratic Convention that nominated Jimmy Carter. I was, as Dick often said, the world's worst assistant.

But life opened up for me. One of the sights I remember was going up to the offices of *New York Magazine* when they were still the center of the New York universe, and there was Clay Felker, a handsome man with a custom-made English candy-striped shirt covering his big belly like a bedsheet, tiny delicate features, big brown eyes, and a voice that was beautiful in its commanding operatic clarity—somewhere between a tenor and a baritone—that started in his chest, with a slight nasality impinging on its tonal purity. Truly, he could have sung instead of speaking and the place would have snapped into shape like a chorus line responding to a Gilbert and Sullivan lead. I was, as so many have been in decades and centuries before in the same circumstances, hooked.

Clay was great, but I would have fallen right in line, I am sure, for the great Ralph Ingersoll or the great Frank I. Cobb or the great Herbert Bayard Swope or dozens of English guys whose names I don't know. They all seem great to we who want to work for them. William Shawn, the most recessive man who ever lived, had a cult.

And Harold Hayes, who ran *Esquire*, spoke. I seem to remember from my brief encounters with him that he was like a Southern cricket with an insatiable need to know. Hayes, handsome and dark, a former Marine, had at least one amazing skill, among others: he was the most intense listener I've ever met. When you spoke to him, he gave you the works, which in his case was impressive, and as a result, you told him everything. If anyone is interested, go back and take a look at my friend Frank DeGiacomo's wonderful piece on the old *Esquire* in *Vanity Fair*. It made me happy because it showed me that Graydon Carter cared. That old *Esquire* crew was the group Clay Felker left to go to the *Herald Tribune*, where he founded *New York Magazine*.

Clay and Hayes and William Shawn and the late editor of *Harper's*, Willie Morris, were very different people, but they were all members of a species missing today: the Neurotic Big City Editor. They were editors who came from out of town to New York, as Ross had. Clay was from St. Louis, Hayes was from North Carolina, Shawn from Chicago, Willie Morris from Mississippi, and they had a need to run the city and its sensibility. They each, as the great editors do, had a topic: Clay's was power, Hayes's was literate American manliness, and Shawn's was deep artistic, socially aware cosmopolitanism. Perhaps none of them created work for the ages, as Faulkner or Hemingway or Fitzgerald or even John O'Hara and John Cheever and John Updike did—there's no Max Perkins biography, probably, of any Shawn, Felker, or Hayes—and in many ways they were at odds. Clay loves to tell a story of Jimmy Breslin, the great columnist, facing down Shawn in a bar over the publication of Tom Wolfe's lacerating piece on *The New Yorker*, the best articulation of battle in the great age of magazines that exists, "Tiny Mummies." Breslin invariably got the best of the exchange in Clay's telling, but Shawn, as far as I'm concerned, looks better and better as the years go on. *The New Yorker* today is a very good magazine but not a very interesting one, and that might well be a reflection of its intelligent but probably not very neurotic editor.

Whereas Harold Ross and Shawn and Luce and Ralph Ingersoll and Sidney Kidd and even the last great outsized big-city editor who came to tame, Tina Brown, were all pretty neurotic, is my guess. For anyone who's interested, Allen Shawn, William Shawn's son, has written an amazing, really funny, and harrowing memoir that has just come out called *Wish I Could Be There*, with an astonishing portrait of his father that tells you exactly why *The New Yorker* was the great magazine it was in the thirty-six years he ran it: "It was perhaps not a coincidence that he worked at a magazine that published its articles without a table of contents for so many years and had its articles signed below the last line rather than after the title, and used, in 'The Talk of the Town' section and in its obituaries, the collective 'we' in place of the undersigned 'I.'"

"The sense that something terrible was about to happen always hovered over my father," wrote Allen Shawn.

And this:

As an editor, he felt free to be himself. Although he felt creatively frustrated and sometimes imagined leading a different life entirely, it was as an editor that he was fully deployed as a personality, intellect, and creative force and that he was dynamic and decisive. Editing involves to a degree censorship and he was already a master of self-censorship. But more importantly, editing is a process of fostering and liberating, freeing both the writer and the writing from whatever holds it back, cutting and pruning and guiding in the service of more exuberant growth. He could free the writing, he could encourage it, he could even help it run wild—but it wouldn't be his. I remember the amazing energy he exuded when I visited him at the magazine, his apple-cheeked complexion, his surprising sociability. There he did not need to go to people. The world's most fascinating people came to him, bringing news of places he would never dream of going to and of things that enthralled him but would be very difficult to investigate first hand. . . . Had he been an inveterate traveler, a doer or a true extrovert, he would have become too jaded and worldly to maintain the striking innocence and almost infinite receptivity that made him capable of listening so raptly and carefully to what writers had to say. Through his work at the magazine he was able to filter the unruly and terrifying world through his own personality without venturing very far. . . . This buried volcano of passions and fears created a surface tension that was palpable.

Shawn was a great man. Quite nuts, maybe, more than anyone knew at the time, but a great man. And his greatness and his nuttiness added up to a lasting monument in the American culture. As had Harold Ross's magazine. "All I do," said Ross, "is cast my bread upon the waters." He may have been being falsely modest, but it's not true. If you look at another case, Harold Hayes, he infused his *Esquire* staff with an idea. And as he tweaked *Esquire* to reflect his vision, Hayes also indoctrinated the staff. "We never wondered what he wanted. We absolutely knew," says John Berendt, who went on to become *Esquire*'s editor-in-chief. And from that came Mailer's "Super Man Goes to the Supermarket," Tom Wolfe's famous assault on the New Left, and the Dubious Achievement Awards that would eventually inspire *Spy* magazine. Beyond journalism, the *Esquire* style seeped into films such as Benton and Newman's *Bonnie and Clyde* and Peter Bogdanovich's *Last Picture Show*.

Clay Felker also laid claim to the New Journalism, but Clay's great invention, it seems to me, was something else: it was the New Ambition. He and Wolfe called New York "The City of Ambition," and part of that was a sense that anything could and ought to happen here, right up to a feeling that a New Yorker, and every *New York Magazine* reader, ought to eat, argue, screw, read, and politic themselves to a point of frenzy particularly because they were New Yorkers. Clay's *New York* showed up in the late '60s, exactly when New York needed it, when New York needed to be reminded it was an amazing place, that it was Paris and Hong Kong combined. Clay and Hayes had battled for control of *Esquire* and Hayes had won and earned posterity, but Clay got the city-state of New York, which he ruled like a czar until Rupert Murdoch took it away from him in a grisly turn of business events in 1977.

What did these guys do that nobody does right now? They inculcated their staff with an idea, with a worldwide view. Clay, Hayes, and Shawn were very different guys, but they infused their staffs with an idea, a worldview, and an aesthetic. I've always believed that the great movie directors do their great work when they are young and full of beans— Orson Welles directed *Citizen Kane* when he was twenty-six, Hawks and Ford and Capa and Wyler were all young when they did their best work. These editors were auteurs as well. It was right up here at Columbia where the *New York Observer*'s film critic, Andrew Sarris, invented the auteur theory and applied it to the great directors. But I really believe it's time to apply an auteur theory to the great magazine editors as well. It's the discipline, the intelligence, the worldview, but also the neurotic disposition of the passionate displacer that makes magazine editing so important: "I can't say it, but you can," he or she says to the writer.

Hayes wasn't a writer until after he left *Esquire*, and Clay was fundamentally a passionate displacer of his energy to his writers. How many times did I sit near his office at *Manhattan, inc.* and hear that voice: "GREEATTT!" even when it wasn't. But it was the passionate, almost childlike sense that he could shake the world that mattered. When I first got to the *Observer*, Clay used to have breakfast with me about once a month at the Peacock Alley at the Waldorf—he chose it—and he would fill me with ideas, more than I could carry in my larder. I once heard Frank Rich describe Arthur Gelb of *The New York Times*, who almost certainly would have been a great magazine editor, "He comes in every morning with 100 ideas, 10 of which are any good." In magazine terms, 10 good ideas is spectacular.

When I got the *Observer*, I sought out Clay, and he was tremendously generous. I leaned on his every word, sure, but more than that was his energy and his enthusiasm that made the day. It was like a kid's or an out-of-towner's. And he understood his idiom. "The *Observer*," he said to me one day, "is a newspaper of interpretation." It may not sound like much to you, but a week doesn't go by when I don't think of it, and how he said it. It was what made his staff love him, the ones that didn't hate him. And you could say the same thing of Hayes and Shawn. They were brilliant, and they never, it seems to me, completely grew up. Yet at the same time, they were as informed and powerful as heads of the state.

There's something else, as Clay used to say: they all loved music. Maybe Clay the least, I don't know, but Shawn was a great jazz pianist. Hayes played the trombone and was a jazz expert. Clay liked to say that a good headline should sound like a song lyric. Okay!

But mostly it was the enthusiasm.

A magazine has to have an idea, and the simpler the better. Clay's New York was the City of Ambition. Ross's *New Yorker* was not for the

Old Lady from Dubuque. Hugh Hefner, another great editor in his own way, created an empire based on one idea: seeing the girl next door naked. Was there anything more American than that? When Henry Luce started *Fortune*, he wanted to use poets on business, and he created, in *Fortune*, one of the greatest of all magazines. And then, within the framework, a staff goes to work, creating—as cinematographers and art directors and editors do for movie auteurs—a world.

At the *New York Observer*, we have a worldview as well, but I won't tell you what it is. Our little newspaper is kind of a hybrid between a magazine and a newspaper. Which means, as Clay said to me, "It's a newspaper of interpretation." "Does it have to be a point-of-view?" he would ask. And what he didn't ask: Was it fun? At the *Observer*, which I will reiterate is just a very little thing, we are redesigning for a new generation. We have a wonderful, brilliant staff. It is to their sweat that I owe almost everything we have. A staff has to understand its paper and love it. It's a living, breathing thing. It is also, I'm happy to report to you, even in 2007, a smoking, drinking thing as well.

They are writers and editors who are committed to creating a written product with literary narrative journalism in a digital, incomplete information age, full of gossips, swift boaters, and hyperbolicists. Even as we redesign our Web site and build a new wireframe, with new servers and the works and the ability to publish electronically simultaneously in Beijing—where our media editor is currently living; Oundle, England—where our books editor lives; and L.A., where our style editor has just moved from, we are still print guys. We are newspaper affirmationists. We are celebrating print. We live among fonts, ink, smudges, and presses. It is our pleasure and our need. Why? We believe it's better that way.

My new owner, whom I like a real lot, is twenty-six and loves the *New York Post*. My old owner, with whom I had lunch every Wednesday like clockwork for ten years, is a book in himself, is seventy-five and likes Saul Bellow and *Grant's Interest Rate Observer*. I am fifty-two, about to turn fifty-three, and a product of these things I'm speaking about, plus *The New York Times*, where I used to work. We have created a hybrid that I hope will work. I think of it as the *New York Post* goes to college. But it is, I hope, very *Observer*ish, true to our values, which include the New

York newspaper tradition, plus these other magazine things I'm speaking about. You'll find parts of newspapers you've never seen in the *New York Observer*: when we first redesigned it, Nancy Butkus and I stole typefaces from the great newspaper of the 1920s, Frank I. Cobb, Herbert Bayard Swope, and Joseph Pulitzer's *New York World*; plus parts of the afternoon liberal iteration of the *New York Post*, where Pete Hamill, Leonard Lyons, and Murray Kempton wrote; plus the *New York Herald-Tribune*, from the corpse of which Clay dragged the live, beating *New York Magazine*. Plus, we've stolen a little bit of the old *Esquire*'s voice, *New York*'s voraciousness, and the old *New Yorker*'s sense that nobody needs to understand it but their readers, and they have no imperative but to be good.

A moment ago I said I wouldn't say what the *Observer* is about, but I will. It's about the social and meritocratic power elite of New York, in politics, in real estate, and in media. It's about climbing on the carcasses of the rich and powerful, as illustrations and stories go back decades and centuries. But their sadness is that they only exist in the moment. Have you ever seen anything staler than last month's *Vanity Fair*? It's true that people save *The New Yorker* in order to never read it, and that attics used to groan and collapse under the weight of *National Geographic*. You should see my office. On the other hand, it's better that you don't. Suffice it to say that it would make the Collier Brothers feel like the Minute Maids. But when I see types and fonts and stories I go a little bonkers and I can't resist them, and it's not just a matter of hitting "Save." There's a front page of *The New York Times* on my floor with a photograph of Bush smirking in his Chinese jacket at a trade conference. I find it irresistible.

And there's the cover of *Esquire* with Richard Nixon that got me into this business in the first place. But the metaphysics of magazines provides a little solace: they don't evaporate into the mist like space signals—they are there to remind us of our passion and our care. They only speak to those who want to listen, but when they do, it's as good as music or art. And when you leave them, it may all finally come down to the headline of one of the greatest magazine profiles ever written, by

Gay Talese in 1966: "Joe, Said Marilyn Monroe, I've Just Come Back form Korea, And You've Never Heard Such Cheering. Yes I Have, Said Joe DiMaggio." We've all just come back from entertaining the troops, and we've all said, "You've never heard such cheering." But yes, they have. And, I hope, yes, you will.

10

The Publisher's Role

Crusading Defender of the First Amendment or Advertising Salesman?

John R. MacArthur has been the president and publisher of *Harper's Magazine* since 1983. Previously, he had been a reporter for *The Wall Street Journal*, the *Washington Star*, *The Bergen Record*, and the *Chicago Sun-Times*, and he was an editor on the foreign desk of United Press International. He served on the board of The Committee to Protect Journalists and is currently a board member at the Authors Guild. MacArthur has written three books: *You Can't Be President: The Outrageous Barriers to Democracy in America* (2008); *Second Front: Censorship and Propaganda in the Gulf War* (1992), which won the Illinois ACLU's 1992 Harry Kalven Freedom of Expression award; and *The Selling of "Free Trade": Nafta, Washington, and the Subversion of American Democracy* (2000). He is also a columnist for *The Providence Journal* and *Le Devoir* (Montreal).

I confess that I've always harbored fantastic and romantic notions about being a magazine or newspaper publisher. At different times in my life, all sorts of preposterous images have presented themselves to me. I'm a raffishly crusading publisher-editor, something like Humphrey Bogart in *Deadline U.S.A.* I'm a patrician publisher, unbought and above reproach, with my somewhat severe oil portrait hanging in the lobby of my building above the ancient and retired Linotype machine. The painting depicts me seated on a desk, my three-piece suit vest elegantly buttoned up, casually holding my publication open across my lap.

I've even seen myself as a mogul publisher, like the sinister Janoth played by Charles Laughton in *The Big Clock*, with many periodicals at my disposal and editors, including Ray Milland, at my beck and call, receiving dignitaries, dispatching politicians to their just reward, moving my chess pieces around the country while hundreds of minions anxiously attempt to interpret my every wink and nod, my every offhand remark.

Now, ranged against these fantasies, unfortunately, has been genuine experience—which began, coincidentally, across the quad over here, in Room 418 of the now-demolished Ferris Booth Hall overlooking Broadway, almost exactly twenty-two years ago. I was just finishing up my year's term as the news editor of the *Columbia Daily Spectator*, and having nothing better to do that evening, agreed to pursue a story that had just been phoned in by a helpful tipster.

It seemed that the grill man at the West End Café, one Ricky Riley, had suddenly had enough of his bosses, or of drunken Columbia students, or of Allen Ginsberg readings—nobody knew for sure. But whatever the trigger was, and long before "Take This Job and Shove It" became a hit song, Mr. Riley allegedly started a fire by pouring a pot of grease on the grill, allegedly stabbed a busboy in the skull, and allegedly rifled the cash register before stalking out onto Broadway, by all accounts unchallenged by the frightened staff and customers. I always liked a good crime story. I loved being able to refer in my lead to a knife-wielding grill man. So I hustled across the street back to the newsroom and duly reported the story.

Now, at some point that night, I got one of the West End's owners on the phone, and to my amazement, he let drop a hint right out of the great unpublished journalism textbook that everyone in our trade knows by heart. "You know," he said, "the West End is a regular advertiser in your newspaper. I'm not sure that your printing this story would really help our business relationship."

This was such a clichéd threat, so heavy-handed and so unexpected, that I was actually quite taken aback, though my twenty-one-year-old bravado didn't permit me to show it. As it was, I simply ignored the warning, then laughed sarcastically about it with my friends, who also laughed. We could afford to. *The Spectator* was virtually a monopoly newspaper and the West End had nowhere else to advertise. As it turned out, the threat was indeed an empty one and the advertising, which was probably worth a few thousand dollars a year, continued without interruption.

Eighteen years later, in 1996, I was sitting at my desk in an office that also overlooks Broadway. But by then I was working much farther downtown and was an actual publisher. I was wearing a suit, though not as elegant as the one I had once imagined, and I was on the phone with the senior vice president for corporate affairs of Pfizer Pharmaceuticals, a gentleman named Constantine Clemente.

I had called him to try and find out exactly why Pfizer had canceled a $100,000 advertising schedule in *Harper's Magazine* before even the first ad had run. I actually knew why. We had just published a very good essay by a wonderful writer named Greg Critser that, among other things, questioned the integrity and ethics of Pfizer and a number of other drug companies in their marketing of antidepressants—including Pfizer's Zoloft.

In the course of this piece, Critser also quoted the chairman of Pfizer in a way intended to be less than flattering. The chairman had told a business journalist that he didn't really need to acquire a managed-care business, which was all the rage at that point, "because we deal with the pharmacy benefit managers. And we have relationships with drugstores. We get wonderful information from drugstores. . . . We can drill down to the patient from any of these centers."

The implication was clear—Pfizer was aggressively, and apparently successfully, trying to bypass pharmacies and doctors to sell Zoloft and other drugs, in effect, directly to the consumer. Mr. Clemente was not happy. "I would expect to see a piece like this in *Mother Jones* or *The Nation*," he hissed to me with barely disguised rage. "Mr. Steere"—the chairman—"was furious, and he personally canceled your advertising contract."

Whew. No clever rejoinders came to mind, so I reached in desperation for a terribly clichéd one. "Well, surely, Mr. Clemente, you don't want to preach to the choir in your advertising, do you?" Silence. "Nice chatting with you, Mr. Clemente."

Now, this was a real pain in the pocketbook for *Harper's*, which is not a rich magazine. If you optimistically assume that Pfizer would have continued to advertise regularly over the next four years and that I also had managed to crack the pharmaceutical manufacturer's trade association ad budget, the Critser article cost us anywhere between $400,000 and a million dollars in revenue—money, I assure you, that would have found many good and timely uses at 666 Broadway. Needless to say, it will be a very long time before *Harper's* sees any drug company advertising.

I tell you this story because despite the growth of the Internet, where in theory anyone can be their own publisher, I remain convinced by A. J. Liebling's famous dictum that freedom of the press is guaranteed only to those who own one. I don't own a printing press, but in effect, I own a title and a copyright and a subscription list. And that's close enough to meeting Liebling's definition of someone with a free-press guarantee.

The *Harper's* name, which, unfunnily enough, is owned by Rupert Murdoch's News Corporation and licensed to us in perpetuity, still packs enough market power to guarantee an audience of several hundred thousand readers. So far I've had no difficulty finding a printer willing to take my money and print my magazine. But without advertising, I'm afraid that many presses would cease to roll and that many magazines, including *Harper's*, would find themselves if not extinguished, then greatly diminished in reach, impact, and freedom.

If you assume, as you should, that the First Amendment is essential to the political health of the country, that it aids and abets the democratic impulse, then you should be greatly concerned by the notion that press freedom nowadays hangs not by a stout cord between publisher and reader, but rather by a more tenuous thread connecting advertisers and the media.

You should also know that this thread is increasingly frayed, and that it is very often pulled by an advertiser with very little interest in the promotion of democracy or the public's so-called right to know. If you want to understand something fundamental about journalism, then you really need to understand something about advertising.

My difficulties with Pfizer were unusual, but not exceptional. The drug companies are particularly aggressive these days. I think that in this respect they're the equivalent of Big Oil in the 1970s and '80s. But other corporations can be similarly heavy-handed. And since advertising dominates the magazine business as never before, this is no small matter for me in my daily rounds. Because the fundamental problem with running a magazine like *Harper's*—or any magazine with ambitions to inform people, rather than just sell stuff—is the dependence on advertising revenue to pay the bills.

Various unfortunate trends have contributed to the worsening of this dependence. One has been the decline of what I would call corporate statesmanship, and its not necessarily unhealthy subsidiary, corporate vanity. Partly because of Ronald Reagan's free market counterrevolution, the deregulation of certain key industries, the general decline of cultural literacy at the highest levels of business, the acceleration of mergers, the stock-market boom, and I suppose the increase in just plain meanness in the marketplace, the top executives at corporations no longer care much what the thoughtful public—especially the traditional civic-minded constituencies like teachers and good government groups—thinks of them. I'm sure you've all noticed that magazines today carry less of what's known as corporate image advertising, which is essentially designed to make the company look nice or friendly or public-spirited to a general audience, and especially to the active-minded intelligentsia.

Roland Marchand's important book on this subject, *Creating the Corporate Soul*, suggests that corporate image advertising was a response to public fears during an earlier wave of corporate mergers, from 1895 to 1904—a period during which, in Naomi Lamoreaux's phrase (which he quotes), the United States was "transformed overnight from a nation of freely competing, individually owned enterprises into a nation dominated by a small number of giant corporations."

These soulless enterprises, as he calls them—soulless in spite of the fact that the Supreme Court had paradoxically recognized them as the equivalent of persons—needed to reassure people that they weren't going to gobble them up or starve them to death.

Marchand writes: "The corporate response took on even more diverse configurations. For instance, a corporation worried about an image of moral irresponsibility might initiate and publicize benefit programs for its employees, associate itself with some current moral or patriotic crusade, or seek to characterize its operations as public service. One dismayed by its apparent lack of personality might erect an impressive new corporate headquarters, disseminate a 'humanized' image of its chief executive, affix a striking logo to all its products, or link its identity with its research laboratories," as AT&T did with Bell Labs, for example.

From 1904 to the early 1980s, this advertising of supposed good works could be counted on to sustain thoughtful magazines and newspapers. And to a remarkable extent, corporate image advertising remained fairly disinterested and apolitical.

Of course, very little media in this country have ever been a threat to corporate power or to the free-market system. Nonetheless, there was a tacit understanding that big corporations shouldn't lean too hard on magazines or newspapers, because if they did, it would probably backfire. Now that this type of advertising has largely given way to much more unsentimental, hard-sell messages designed only to move products or stock or raise the stock price, a whole class of very thoughtful, well-educated corporate middlemen and -women has been nearly wiped out.

Whatever you think of their career choices or the ethical compromises they made within these companies, this class of corporate statesmen and do-gooders was much better for me and for the media—and very possibly for the country—than the people who have come after, including the supposedly free-spirited Internet tycoons.

Now, I don't want to exaggerate. Most of the better P.R. and advertising types I came to know in the '80s worked for heavily regulated industries that were highly dependent on the favor of politicians—especially AT&T before it was broken up; premerger defense contractors like McDonnell-Douglas, Rockwell International, Northrop, and Grumman; and major New York banks like Citibank and Bankers Trust.

Of course these people wanted to stay on the good side of the readers of *Harper's*, *The New Yorker*, *The Atlantic*, *The New Republic* and *The Nation*, because these readers included national politicians and their staff members—not to mention countless school board members and principals and their ultimate bosses in state or county legislatures.

Even in today's degraded intellectual environment, these magazines are still a good way to reach the nation's political leaders. Dick Morris, Bill Clinton's disgraced political strategist, wrote in his memoir that "if you wanted your views to reach the President, the way to do it was through the op-ed pages of *The New York Times* and *The Washington Post* or through articles in *Harper's*, *The New Yorker*, *The New Republic*, *The Atlantic* and a few other magazines." At a White House press conference promoting the Democratic plan to increase the minimum wage, the then-House Minority Leader, Richard Gephardt, went on at length describing a *Harper's* piece by Barbara Ehrenreich about how hard it was to get by on the current minimum wage.

But there are very few people left in corporations with the inclination to place ads that would reach the supposedly influential political types. Presumably they think that corporate political action committees are a more efficient way to reach politicians. I'm not sure.

The old-school corporation P.R. men were mostly ex-newspaper reporters with guilty consciences. They felt guilty for having switched sides, for the money, the security, the regular hours. Or they were former advisors to politicians with some genuine interest in public affairs and the civic health of the nation.

I'll never forget my first lunch in Los Angeles with Les Daly, a reporter-turned-VP of Public Affairs at Northrop, which was in hot competition with General Dynamics, McDonnell-Douglas, and Grumman for air force and navy fighter-bomber contracts during the big Reagan military buildup. I was trying to sell him space and, assuming him to be a scheming cynic and tool of the military-industrial complex, I was actually afraid of sounding too idealistic about *Harper's*, or what I viewed as *Harper's* educational and civic mission.

So in passing, I made some kind of self-deprecating or ironic remark about *Harper's* efforts to defend the First Amendment, simply to avoid looking like a moralizing do-gooder. "Never joke about freedom of the press," he told me. "It's too important." He was visibly angry with me for joking about it.

Thus, in those days, *Harper's* could hammer away at the Reagan administration, the defense contractors, the reactionary right—just about everybody in power but the individual CEOs, perhaps—and be protected by the Les Dalys of the corporate world from having the advertising pulled. If we did publish something negative about an advertiser, as a courtesy we would simply call them in advance and allow them to pull their ad in that issue, and then the advertising would resume the following month.

We even got a Pfizer ad in those enlightened days, placed in the magazine by a very fine fellow named Chuck Frye. Chuck happened to be a liberal-minded former CIA analyst and—I don't think coincidentally—the son and grandson of International Typographical Union officers in Denver. On certain days, he seemed even more suspicious of government, big business, and politicians than I was. He was a man of great sophistication. He knew more about opera than anyone I've ever met. His kind has virtually ceased to exist in the upper echelons of the Fortune 500.

But again, I don't want to exaggerate. Another very sophisticated corporate public relations liberal named Herb Schmertz—he of *Masterpiece Theater* and the Mobil op-ed ads in *The New York Times*—encouraged Mobil's president, William Tavoulareas, in 1977 to sue Lewis Lapham, my editor, and *Harper's* for libel, if you can believe this, for describing him in a column as "red-faced," "choleric," and a "representative of the merchant class."

That this lawsuit was destined to fail does nothing to diminish its brazen and bullying contempt for freedom of the press. As I said, Big Oil was the pharmaceutical business of the 1970s. But Schmertz and Mobil were the exception, not the rule. His counterparts at other corporations were far more interested in making friends than making enemies in the press.

The ultimate bosses, the CEOs for the most part, were literate though limited men who had some modicum of respect for the serious press. Or if they didn't, were taught by their P.R. men to pretend that they did. Walter Wriston, the former chairman of Citibank, was, after all, the son of the onetime president of Brown University. And he still seemed to believe that serious magazines and newspapers mattered. Or at least he talked a good game. And so did his P.R. man, the late Will Sparks, who worked in politics for President Johnson.

I know this will horrify you, but George Weissman, former chairman of Philip Morris, a loyal supporter of *Harper's Magazine*, went on to be chairman of Lincoln Center and was possibly the only CEO in America to support George McGovern's candidacy for president in 1972. Whatever you think of the tobacco business, however self-interested you might think him, this was a thoughtful, fairly public-spirited man, as was his successor, Hamish Maxwell.

Occasionally, I came across corporate P.R. men who were quite brilliant. One of them, Jerry Meyer of McDonnell-Douglas, was eventually punished for his intelligence and integrity and quite brutally downsized. He wrote a wonderful book about this experience called *Executive Blues*. But the bottom line is, there's no room left in Big Business for the Jerry Meyers of the world.

I've dwelled at some length on advertising because it takes up much of my time and because the situation's only getting worse. But you can't just blame the change in the political and educational culture inside corporations for the deteriorating climate. Advertisers today throw their weight around more than ever because they've been invited to do so by the publishers.

With the advent in the 1970s of so-called advertorials—that is, advertising promotion copy masquerading as real editorial material—the walls between advertising and editorial have weakened apace. Labeled advertorial has more and more been supplanted by unlabeled advertorial, where the editor is called upon to run articles complementary to the adjacent advertising.

We call these things adjacencies. Whereas before, a publisher was obliged to call an advertiser only to warn them about an editorial adjacency that might embarrass them so that the advertiser could withdraw from that particular issue, today a publisher is virtually obliged to inform the advertiser of a favorable editorial adjacency as part of an implicit bargain when the advertiser buys the space.

Advertisers have been emboldened to take greater and greater liberties—not only by the Reagan revolution but also by the media. I blame Si Newhouse in particular because of what he has done to *The New Yorker*, which was for many years—if I may borrow a phrase from the Japanese—the magazine that could say no.

The New Yorker, because of its advertising dominance among magazines—in one year in the mid-1960s it carried more than 6,000 pages of advertising—could essentially dictate terms to advertisers. The wall between advertising and editorial was so high and thick that the longtime editor, William Shawn, would occasionally reject advertising on grounds of taste and aesthetics.

When Newhouse bought the magazine in 1985—a purchase, by the way, that I unavailingly protested to the then-owner, Peter Fleischmann—the wall began to crumble. The new Condé Nast-trained management began introducing Special Advertising Sections filled with nonsensical advertorial copy. They staged special advertising events that made fools of *The New Yorker* writers in front of the advertising community.

The most depressing example was a make-believe press conference in which Dick Morris, then at the peak of his disgraced, toe-sucking celebrity, answered questions from three *New Yorker* writers before a private audience composed exclusively of advertisers. This was bad enough, but even worse, Morris's answers were off the record. So whatever thin journalistic pretext existed for the event was completely undermined.

Of course, the caving of *The New Yorker* has only made my life more difficult, something I must have anticipated when I protested to Fleischmann way back in '85. Before, if an advertiser demanded advertorial or special editorial adjacencies or anything else untoward or unethical, I could politely refuse, and for good measure say, "Well, *The New Yorker* wouldn't do it either." Now I couldn't say that anymore. Not only did *The New Yorker* do it, they did it more aggressively than a lot of other, less prestigious magazines.

I am reliably informed that *The New York Times* is arguing internally about advertorial. They're already happy to publish special sections solely designed to attract advertising. But I know of one instance three years ago where an editor of a regular news section in the Sunday paper was asked to assign an upbeat story about restaurants in a certain neighborhood that would run adjacent to ads for some of those restaurants. The editor protested to Gene Roberts, the then-managing editor of the *Times* and a man of great integrity. Roberts did the right thing and squashed the incipient unlabeled advertorial. But I fear that he was holding his finger in the dike. [Editor's note: The *Times*, did, eventually start running advertorials, albeit online in special sections.]

If I can digress just slightly, I'll relate an anecdote about just how brutal consumer magazines can be in their pursuit of advertising. The late Liz Tilberis, who edited *Harper's Bazaar* quite brilliantly, fought cancer and *Vogue* with equal determination, and she almost succeeded in surviving both enemies. She once told me a story about a major fashion advertiser who recounted a conversation he had had with Steve Florio, the president of Condé Nast and the onetime publisher of *The New Yorker*, and his sidekick, Ron Galotti, the then-publisher of *Vogue*.

Vogue had long been the dominant fashion magazine. But Liz and *Harper's Bazaar* were starting to make some inroads after five years of persistence. According to Liz, the advertiser had told his visitors that he admired what she was doing at *Bazaar* and that he was thinking of placing a schedule in the magazine. "What do you want to advertise in her magazine for?" one of the two salesmen was said to have protested. "She's dying of cancer."

Tough stuff, raw stuff.

There's another important factor that's made magazines more vulnerable to the demands and whims of advertisers, which is the continuing decline in the cost of subscriptions. Because magazines are so desperate for advertising, they view subscribers by and large as loss leaders whose principal function is to support the publication's guaranteed advertising rate base. Since the advertising agencies get a flat percentage of whatever they buy—traditionally it's 15 percent—the more the page costs, the more they make. Thus publishers and ad directors of magazines strain mightily and discount heavily to make their circulation as big as possible in order to please the ad agencies.

Thus, it has gotten cheaper and cheaper to subscribe to magazines, which makes it harder for magazines like *Harper's*, which simply cannot get as much advertising as, say, *Vanity Fair*, to charge a decent price for its editorial matter. Price sensitivity among subscribers is extreme. Just a dollar increase can sharply lower response to subscription offers and renewal offers.

At the same time, the Internet—with its implied promise of free, free, free editorial content—encourages people to think that they shouldn't have to pay for magazines and newspapers at all. To my mind, the Internet is just a gigantic, much-faster version of the photocopying machine. And as such, it is a great enemy of periodicals, because so many library users and professors are happy to read a cheap Xerox of an article or distribute it to their students, rather than pay for a subscription. I've tried again and again to explain to the young Internet enthusiasts on my staff that the Web is actually driving down the perceived value of their work, which makes us even more dependent on advertising.

In any event, low-cost or no-cost subscriptions just make magazines hostages to the advertisers. What we need is readers who are willing to take back more of the burden of subsidizing the media—especially the serious media.

Now, I know that I've painted a fairly grim picture of my job, and I don't want to exaggerate about that either. You must understand that I'm a reporter at heart and my reporter's heart, combined with my publisher's authority, often provides me with great amusement and enormous satisfaction. Pfizer may have yanked their ad schedule, but our piece got the Food and Drug Administration to send Pfizer's chairman a warning letter about Pfizer's promotional materials and activities for the marketing of Zoloft.

Among other things, the letter said that Pfizer was "disseminating promotional materials for Zoloft that promote unapproved uses and that contain statements, suggestions or implications that are false, lacking in fair balance or otherwise misleading in violation of the Federal Food, Drug, and Cosmetic Act," et cetera. And they told them to cut it out.

This sort of outcome is a very gratifying part of my job. What's more, the next time a negative piece pops up in *Harper's* about the drug business, I'll be able to promote it happily and with absolutely no ambivalence or fear of reprisal. One of the nice things about being a publisher, if you're so inclined, is that if someone leans on you the wrong way, you can lean back with some force.

Nevertheless, *Harper's* needs advertising to be strong, and I cannot emphasize enough the danger inherent in that need. I can see the day when the big media corporations and advertisers finally just dispense with the formalities and simply merge their staffs. You know, "This article was sponsored by Pfizer with the help of Pfizer's scientists."

As the price publishers and readers are willing to pay for genuine writing and reporting continues to fall, pushed by the Internet and by publications increasingly subsidized by advertisers with no interest in real journalism, I suspect that more and more freelancers will be driven out of business and more and more media will be staff-written, with all the blandness and compromises that inevitably result from committee journalism.

The staff writer, you must remember, as well as the staff editor, must always be looking over their shoulder for the guys from the advertising department, whereas the freelancer tends to be freer to think about the journalistic task at hand. To the freelancer, advertising is the publisher's problem—that is, my problem—which is the way things ought to be.

11

Editing Books Versus Editing Magazines

Robert Gottlieb, editor and writer, was the editor-in-chief of Simon and Schuster and Alfred A. Knopf. From 1987 to 1992 he was the editor-in-chief of *The New Yorker*. He has since published *Reading Jazz* (1999), a collection of jazz autobiographies, reportage, and criticism; coedited the anthology *Reading Lyrics* (2000); and written *George Balanchine: The Ballet Maker* (2004) and *Sarah: The Life of Sarah Bernhardt* (2010). His essays include dance and book reviews for *The New York Observer* as well as book reviews for *The New Yorker*, *The New York Review of Books*, and *The New York Times Book Review*. Robert Gottlieb spoke on February 21, 2002.

I'm not a journalist, and my only connection to journalism was the six years that I was the editor of *The New Yorker* magazine, where there was a lot of journalism, but of a different kind than most. So I'm not sure that my experience there as an editor is typical of the experience of most editors who work with journalists.

So I am primarily a book editor, and most of what I can tell you has to do with what [editing] can achieve at its best and what it can screw up at its worst, which it often is.

Editors do different things in different places. To start with, being the editor-in-chief of a book publishing house is a vastly different matter from being the editor-in-chief of a magazine. When you're in a publishing house, you are in a strictly service job as an editor. Your job is to serve the book and the writer. You may think you're the star, particularly if various newspapers are writing feature journalism about where you have lunch, but that is not the point.

The point is that book publishing houses only exist with the goodwill of their writers and only exist if the books they publish are any good. To keep your good authors and to attract other good authors, you have to serve them. They have to feel protected, which means they have to believe that their editor, a specific personal editor, understands their work, sympathizes with their work, and is on their wavelength. They must believe that the editor can help them make the book not other than what it is, but better than what it is. And that's a complicated job, and it's a job that can't be taught and can't be learned. I've always thought I was as good or even better as an editor my first day on the job—when I had a lot of energy—as I am now, forty-six years later or so.

You are there to keep the writer happy and feeling that he or she is protected both in terms of writing and in terms of publishing, and publishing and editing are very different matters. I, who would rather do a lot of things pretty well than one thing very well, published as well as edited, and that was fun for me. At that time, you could still be the chief editor and the publisher of a major publishing house. That is much harder to do today because it is a more bottom-line business and accountants and lawyers are far more involved than they used to be.

Anyway, as the editor-in-chief—or just an editor—at a publishing house, you live in terror of disaffecting your writers, because you know what? There are a lot of other publishing houses, and if Toni Morrison or Robert Caro or Joe Heller or John Cheever or Barbara Tuchman or John le Carré—I'm just trying to think of people I've worked with—if they don't like what I'm doing, everybody else is very eager to sign them up.

So editors live in real trepidation of how writers feel about us, and that is a very, very healthy relationship, in my view. But sometimes we get swell-headed, and certainly, in my early days, I could be very contentious and fight with a writer for twenty minutes about a semicolon because I knew the truth and he didn't and it was my job to explain that to him, not always tactfully.

I learned that not every semicolon was crucial, and that there was only so much you could do with a writer; you could take him or her as far as you could, and then there came a point when either the writer or you could go no further. The book was done, and that was it, with all its flaws.

It is always the books, by the way, that you spend the most time on and put the most editorial energy into that get reviews that say, "What this book needed was a good editor." And that's for a reason. Because when a book is really in trouble, there's a point beyond which you can't go. And some reviewers, not all, are slow to catch on to that.

When you're the editor-in-chief of a magazine, as I was of *The New Yorker*, it's opposite. You are the living god. You are not there to please the writers, but the writers are there to satisfy you because they want to be in the magazine, and you are the one who says yes or no. And if it was *The New Yorker* there was basically nowhere else to go. If you were the kind of writer who needed to be in *The New Yorker*, who wanted to be in *The New Yorker*, or wanted an extended lifetime relationship with *The New Yorker*, you had to please the editor, whether it was Harold Ross or William Shawn or myself or Tina Brown or now, David Remnick.

When I first got there, I was really horrified by this attitude. I found it very distasteful that writers were trying to please me rather than to have me trying to please them. And I really didn't know how to handle that. I was also horrified because Mr. Shawn, who was then seventy-nine, had been there so long and was so venerated that on top of being the editor-in-chief of *The New Yorker* he really was a living god there and was treated as such.

Shawn also had—and this is indiscreet—a genius for passive aggression that didn't hurt this dynamic at the magazine. I did not like this at all, and it took me a long time, a) to get used to it, and b) to convince people that far from being a living god, I was just the slob that they saw running around the office talking too much. In fact, there was a wonderful moment after I had been there about six months when my closest colleague said to me—he also had been quite nervous with me—"You know, people keep coming to me and saying, 'I just ran into Bob in the hall. He said so-and-so; what do you think he meant?'" And my colleague said it took him about six months before he was able to say with a certain calm authority that probably what I had meant was what I said, because he himself was a graduate of the particular madhouse that *The New Yorker* has been. What was said in Mr. Shawn's day was not always what was meant. There were signs and omens, and then you tried to study the entrails and figure out what was actually being thought by Mr. Shawn.

Anyway, I finally got used to being a living god, but that aspect of the job continued to bother me. What didn't bother me, and what I came to love—although at first I was confused by it—was the methods of *The New Yorker* at that time. Here again, there was a tremendous difference from book publishing. Think of it this way: a normal book publishing house like Knopf publishes 130, 140 books a year, that can each be 200, 500, or 800 pages long. And they go through many versions and every book is different. You're inventing the wheel with every book, 150 times a year. What that means is that there's a lot there isn't time for.

For instance, no book publishers have checking departments. We can't. If you write a book on seventeenth-century American history, 630 pages long, there is no way that the publishing house can check you. That is, as we say, "on the author."

In the same way, copyediting and proofreading is mostly freelance, and its quality varies (although certainly Knopf, and a number of other publishing houses, still have very effective copyediting and proofreading departments.) And I can say that although I've been embarrassed by some of the books we've published, on the whole we've done a good job. Certainly better than most publishing houses, and certainly better than any British publishing houses, since I really don't believe an editor or a copyeditor's pencil has ever touched a piece of text in England. It's really amazing what they do not do, but then they love amateurism.

Now, when I got to *The New Yorker* I encountered a system so complicated, so obsessive, and so brilliant that after I got over being both confused and dazzled by it, I really did fall in love with it. *The New Yorker* is probably the only place in the world where that happened and/or happens, and it is some kind of shining ideal unless it drives you crazy, and then you shouldn't be working at *The New Yorker* or writing for it.

There were levels and levels of readership on the staff of the magazine. The editor-in-chief, which when I was there was myself, received all the manuscripts that were assigned. They didn't come to the writer's specific editor. They came to the editor-in-chief because, remember, he was the god. So he got a manuscript, and he would read it—I would read it—Shawn would read it—Tina, whoever—and would then assign it to an editor (unless he was going to edit it himself).

Usually the writers had their own editors. John Updike always had the same editor. Most of the writers had a regular editor. So there was a continuing relationship between writer and editor, although officially, any writer could be assigned to any editor. The editor would then do a cut. I—the editor-in-chief—sometimes read it again if I was not the editor myself, and then it would be set in type, and after it was set in type, in the old days, it was left in type. Days went by, weeks went by. Months went by. Sometimes years went by, and there were occasions when decades went by. There it sat in type, waiting to be put on the publishing schedule.

When the editor finally decided to schedule it and run it, the piece "emerged" from where it was, and it was then distributed to many people. The chief among those people, other than the editor, was a fact-checker, and as everybody knows, *The New Yorker* was particularly obsessed with fact-checking. Now, if it was a nonfiction piece, it went to a woman named Eleanor Gould, known familiarly as Miss Gould. Miss Gould, whom I finally got up the nerve to call Eleanor, was an utterly extraordinary machine. She had edited every "fact" piece published in the magazine since she joined it.

She attacked every piece with her little fine pencil in an obsessive way and in blinders. She knew nothing about style. It didn't interest her. What interested her were grammar, accuracy, and clarity. Taste was not an issue. Eleanor was never allowed even to look at fiction, because to tell the truth, she had a tin ear. But on nonfiction, she was a genius.

The first piece I edited for the magazine was by a very young new writer, Caroline Alexander (who since wrote the big best-seller *The*

Endurance). Caroline had never before written for the magazine, and Eleanor had never seen her prose before. It was a dangerous combination.

I received a proof. It was about 50 or 60 galleys—pieces that long don't run in the magazine anymore—and every inch of both sides and the top and the bottom of the galley was covered with this tiny little scroll, with arrows, and different comments were interlinked with other comments. The first week I couldn't even look at it. When I finally started to work on it, I couldn't do more than two galleys a day, and I thought she was mad.

She *was* mad. But she was great. And the more I studied what Eleanor did, the more I came to understand what the basis of *The New Yorker* approach to writing was, which was not, as in a book publishing house, "We're going to do our best to improve this piece." That was a forbidden word at *The New Yorker*: you were never supposed to "improve" writing. What you were supposed to do was correct it, and that's what Eleanor did.

So Eleanor had what was called the Gould Proof. Strong men trembled at the idea of receiving a Gould Proof, and very few writers were allowed to even see their Gould Proofs because their egos would not have survived. John Updike did see his Gould Proof, always, and he and Eleanor had a quite amusing written relationship because he prided himself, quite rightly, on his brilliance as a grammarian and as an accurate writer, and I think she quite enjoyed finding ways of sticking it to him. So there'd be a proof and he would write in the margin, "Oh, let's give Eleanor her parentheses," meaning "She got me." But to show you how brilliant she was, I was one day working with Susan Sontag on her first piece at *The New Yorker*, and she wanted to see the Gould Proof. She had heard about the Gould Proof, and although she's an amiable person, really doesn't like being corrected. I have to tell you that.

We were looking at the Gould Proof, and there wasn't a great deal because she was a clean writer, but at every point she would bristle and say, "Ah, wait, I don't understand this, why is she making this change?" Halfway through the galleys, Susan—who is also very, very smart—really did a doubletake. She said, "Wait a minute, this woman is a genius. She's completely brilliant. I want her to edit everything of mine. I've got to go and tell her. I've got to go and thank her."

Eleanor Gould by this time had gone stone deaf overnight, so that now one could only communicate with her through notes. So Susan ran into her office and wrote out her congratulations to Eleanor.

Besides the Gould Proof, there was the copyeditor's proof. Then there was the checker's proof, the editor's proof, the writer's proof, and if I was not the editor myself, the editor had my proof. So there were six proofs to reconcile.

Into the editor's office would come the writer, if he or she was in town; the checker; and the OKer, whose job was to take all the solutions that were agreed upon among these six disparate proofs and write them in on a master proof. These sessions could be lengthy, but what they led to was a kind of fantasy of accuracy, an intense pursuit of excellence, if this is what excellence meant to you.

I, who had never had the luxury of doing this as a book editor, was completely captivated by it, and that was the part of the job that I liked the most, sitting there with these six proofs and these crazy people trying to work it out. And it did work out.

There were difficult moments, such as the night that had the latest closing in *The New Yorker* history, as I remember. It was at the point when Robert Bork had been nominated for the Supreme Court and one of our writers (whom it is tactless to name, but was Renata Adler) had written a very extended piece condemning the Bork nomination—quite appropriately, as far as I was concerned—and I decided that we would give the entire "Talk of the Town" section, which included "Comment" (as we called the "Notes and Comment" section), to this piece. In those days, "Talk of the Town" and "Comment" were anonymous. So whoever wrote them was not speaking for him- or herself but was speaking for *The New Yorker*, which meant that we had to pay particular attention to everything there.

Well, Renata had a long feud with the chief checker, another adorable but demented person, and they barely spoke to each other. So there we are in my office, myself and the OKer and Ms. Gould and the chief checker and Renata. And the chief checker started attacking Renata's accuracy and Renata, let's say, was not too pliable. The situation got worse and worse, angrier and angrier.

In any case, we finally ended at two in the morning, after about eight hours of working on this piece. But you'll be glad to know that when I said to Miss Gould—who was then in her seventies—"Eleanor, don't come in tomorrow morning, it's so late," she said, "What do you mean? I love this. The happiest time in my life has been since my husband died and I don't have to worry about when I can come in to work or not come in to work." That was Eleanor.

Anyway, this process was very thrilling and very beautiful, and it's still beautiful, and I think Tina Brown respected it. David Remnick certainly respects it. And many of the people who were doing it then and who were doing it for Mr. Shawn are still doing it.

So, that's *The New Yorker*. Now, I can also tell you, as a sort-of writer, what it's like to be edited.

I write for three publications: *The New York Times Book Review* that was in recent years edited by the person who was my deputy at *The New Yorker*, Charles "Chip" McGrath; *The New York Observer*, where I write both dance and book reviews; and *The New York Review of Books*.

All of my editors are old friends of mine. But the dynamics between them and me are completely different in each case, because these editors are focused on different kinds of things. I don't believe there is such a thing as "the editor–author relationship." Of the hundreds of writers with whom I have dealt as a book publisher, there were really no two cases that were the same. Different writers need different things. The editor's job is to intuit, somehow, what those things are.

For instance, sometimes the most important thing you can do for a writer, you do before the book is even written. An example: after Toni Morrison wrote her second novel, *Sula*—which is a wonderful short book—I said, "You know, Toni, *Sula* is a perfect book, it's like a sonnet, you don't have to do that again. You're free to open yourself up and write a more expansive book and take bigger chances, even if it doesn't work. Go for it."

Well, I wasn't telling her anything she didn't know. She knew what she was capable of. But as her editor and publisher, I was in a way not just encouraging her, but freeing her to do what she wanted to do. And that next book was *Song of Solomon*, which indeed was her breakthrough book.

The other thing I could do for her at that point (and I know this is vulgar because it's about money), was to say to her, "Don't worry about money. Your agent and I will worry about it. You can give up your job at Random House if you want to stop editing and just be the writer you are." She didn't do that immediately, but again, she needed that support.

Now, that doesn't mean that when Toni wrote *Song of Solomon* I didn't give the usual comments or do cosmetic editing of one kind or another. I did, and we had a good time with it. But anybody could have done that. My help to her was in liberating her, telling her it was all right to go forward in the way she knew she had to go.

So what was my job there as an editor? I wasn't editing. I was just talking to someone I knew well and saying what I really believed.

Now in other cases, it's exactly the opposite. You sit there for week after week, month after month, wrestling with text. For instance, with Robert Caro's first book, *The Power Broker* (which won the Pulitzer Prize), the great book about New York City, the text was originally 1,100,000 words long. It didn't have to be.

So I worked on that text for a year, and eventually together we cut 450,000 words. In other words, three longish novels were out of that book. This is an exaggeration, but you'll excuse it: every one of those words was a battleground. It was tough because Bob is a believer and I'm a believer, and we locked horns and we were both younger. Now we've just finished working on three more books. He's been working on his Lyndon Johnson biography and just finished volume three. We managed to get through this editing in a year, but there were no quarrels really, just the odd horrible moments. We've both come to accommodate each other and to understand how we could work with each other to make it better. But that's a different relationship from any I've had, with anybody else.

The novelist Doris Lessing is one of my closest friends (although I no longer publish her because when I left for *The New Yorker*, she left Knopf). Doris has for decades—whether I was her publisher or not—sent me her manuscripts the moment she's finished them, and I'd tell her what I think. She would say, "What do you think, what do you think? I'm eager to know what you think." And I would tell her what I thought and she'd say, "That's so interesting." And that was the end of the story.

So once I said to her, "Doris, I don't mind—my ego is not involved here—but why do you want my opinion when you show no signs of making any use of it?" She said, "But don't you understand? I've so much hope for your approval." Now, this is from someone who is considered a breakthrough feminist. So, I don't know, make of it what you will. She claims that she does listen to me, but I say that is not so.

I was only scared of a writer once, and that was of John Cheever, who came to me late in his career. I thought, *Who am I to tell John Cheever that the end of his novel is wrong?* And that was hard, because I did admire him so. And I finally had to sit myself down and say, *Look, he came to Knopf because he wanted you as an editor, and besides, giving your opinion to writers is what they pay you all that money for, so you'd better do it*, and I got my courage up and told him what I thought, and he said, "Sure, fine." Type, type, type, and he fixed it. Somebody else could have gone through the roof. You have to take your chances, because that's your job.

12

The Reader Is King

Felix Dennis is the owner of Dennis Publishing, which publishes about fifty magazines, including *The Week*. In his boisterous career and life, he has been: a successful and pioneering publisher of magazines on such topics as computers and martial arts, as well as the successful "lad mag" *Maxim*; a defendant in a conspiracy trial during his time as coeditor of the allegedly obscene *Oz* magazine in Britain; a crack cocaine addict; and one of the best-selling poets in the United Kingdom. He takes pride in having written the first printed review of the first Led Zeppelin album. Felix Dennis's talk was delivered on April 17, 2008.

You cannot hope
to bribe or twist,
thank God! the British
journalist.

But, seeing what
the man will do
unbribed, there's
no occasion to.

You may think that Humbert Wolfe was being as harsh as he was chauvinistic when he penned those lines in the 1920s. Well, perhaps; but Rebecca West didn't think so. As a novelist and prolific contributor to magazines and newspapers, she had a verdict on your chosen profession even more damning: "Journalism—an ability to meet the challenge of filling the space."

I might add that she omitted the essential rider to this definition: "on time and on budget!" Not that her omission surprises me—certainly not after forty years of experience in magazine publishing. Some of the most inventive journalism I've encountered has been encapsulated in the editorial expense reports of journalists, which, for some mysterious reason, often involve a copious medicinal use of alcohol and the upgrading of airline seating arrangements.

Now, to get down to brass tacks. I intend to limit my heretical advice to you, thrusting and dynamic tyros (upon whose shoulders the future of our industry rests, God help us), to only three main points, the first of which arises from a conversation I had recently with a person who teaches journalism for a living.

Our discussion centered on what I ought to talk to you about today. I regret to say that I found her suggestions unhelpful. They sounded like Tony Blair at a meeting of the British Women's Institute: all spin and grin instead of jam and gin. There was a lot of use of the word "innovation." Personally, I've never been too keen on innovation. Here's a gem of a quote on the subject from an academic scribbler, Malcolm Bradbury: "Reading someone else's newspaper or magazine is like sleeping with someone else's wife. Nothing seems to be precisely in the right place, and when you find what you're looking for, it's not clear how to respond to it."

Bradbury's wit conceals a fundamental truth: familiarity is a vital weapon in the armory of virtually all periodicals and magazines, a kind of armor against direct competitors and other forms of media. I can think of a score of magazines (one or two of my own among them) which gainfully employ large numbers of editors and journalists (and the parasites they carry on their back), solely because their readers just can't get around to canceling their subscription.

Readers on the whole don't want innovation. They don't want to know what a clever dick you are. Think of Al Gore, perhaps the brightest dunce who ever walked the planet and lost the presidency.

What they want in their magazines is just about the same, for any magazine anywhere in the world: they want to be informed and entertained simultaneously, in a familiar format. So be cautious before you rush around advocating the ripping up of blueprints. Judicious evolution is usually preferable to editorial revolution.

So, heresy number one. Until you have mastered your craft, keep your opinions to yourself when you write. Only clapped-out journalists and hacks peddle opinions masquerading as news or fact. Amusing as they may occasionally be, they're not a good role model for young journalists on their way to becoming newspaper, magazine, or Web editors. Entertain. Inform. And beware of show-off innovation.

Bearing in mind exceptions which will readily spring to your minds—the kind of columnist who commands a six-figure salary—I would like to suggest to you that entertaining, well-researched, and informative writing will get the job done in 99 cases out of 100. And getting the job done, issue after issue, is crucial. Consistency and stamina count in our business.

My second subject concerns the threat the Internet poses to the magazine industry generally. In a nutshell, my advice to you is . . . relax.

Much has been written and a great deal of hot air expended on the threat that the Internet supposedly poses to those of us who make a living smearing hieroglyphics on paper. Most of it is so partisan that it can be difficult to tell the wood from the trees. The good news is that I've lived in that forest, making an excellent living there, for a very long time indeed. During the infancy of the Web, decade or more ago, my company came to two crucial conclusions. First, we refused to throw money in a blind panic at this new technology. Instead, we would grow our Web presence as the Web grew. We would make it pay. That was a brave decision at a time when larger publishers were running around like chickens with their heads chopped off, chucking shareholders' money at a medium which had no earthly chance of repaying their investment—for the simple reason that there were so few advertisers on the Web.

Second, we concluded that the Web should not be treated as merely an extension of our ink-on-paper brands and products. It was a beast of a different stripe. This was a counterintuitive conclusion back then (remember AOL/Time-Warner corporate "synergy"?), but we persevered and permitted our Web editors and journalists to break away early from the domination of the "mother ship" ink-on-paper brand and develop their own Internet identity. In retrospect, this was possibly the best decision made by my board in decades.

Now, it may true that we are in the autumn of the glory days of ink on paper. But as far as writers, journalists, and editors are concerned, the growing power and reach of the Internet represents nothing but good news. Possibly the best news for a long time.

Not only does the Web represent a completely new marketplace for all of you, its so-called threat to ink on paper will have little effect on your employment and earning prospects. All it requires is a change of mind-set—and the young are very good at that. Even if, in years to come, the convergence of Web, downloadable video, and television technology has seriously eroded the ink-on-paper marketplace, well-trained journalists and writers like yourself will be perfectly placed to earn a decent crust.

Please remember to toss a few coins into the hat of the fat bearded idiot with glasses you will find manning the last newsstand in New York. I began my career selling magazines on King's Road in London, so I will be perfectly prepared to retreat to my Jurassic roots. From street magazine seller to street magazine seller in a fifty-year career.

For you young geniuses, I assume that there is no intrinsic, visceral bonding to ink on paper. Many of you may already have come to think of yourselves as content providers—and to hell with the medium you provide. That's fine.

But it's different for us old-timers. You have never stood at midnight, half drunk from the hospitality of your print-account handler, dwarfed in the vast cathedral of a printing plant, your head dizzy from the fumes of ink and acetone, marveling at the roar and thundering power of giant paper reels and a machine an eighth of a mile in circumference as it spews out hundreds of thousands of copies of your baby into the waiting arms of binding machines. And, I suspect, very few of you will ever do so . . . more's the pity. Forgive my digression.

I repeat: talent rules. Talent, allied to craft, is the one-eyed prince in the land of the blind. And what *is* inspired talent and craft in our industry, after all, but the application of the seat of the pants to the seat of the chair. (I pinched that from another American journalist: Mark Twain.)

So, heresy number two. Magazines and newspapers are great training grounds, and while changes in technology and media preference may well beggar old-style twentieth-century publishers, put their production and circulation departments in the poorhouse, and bankrupt national distributors and printing companies, *journalists, writers, and editors will still be employed at vastly inflated salaries, because the media can't exist without them.* Talent, allied to craft, rules. It will always rule. So, congratulations on choosing a career with the brightest of prospects which, from a technological standpoint, is virtually bulletproof and futureproof. Now what?

Now we come to the third of my subjects today: making money in publishing by remembering one cardinal fact—the reader is king. I will say it again—the reader is king. You will hear that platitude often in the mouths of American media owners, but you know what? A great many of them speak with forked tongue. I will not go so far as to call them liars, but I will state, categorically and publicly, that they are economical with the truths they hold in their secret heart. To quote Winston Churchill a hundred years ago in the British House of Commons, whre politicians are not permitted to call other members of Parliament liars, they are guilty of a terminological inexactitude. And, most certainly, they do not practice what they preach. To many of them, the king is dead. Screw the reader. The advertiser rules. Long live the king.

What right do I have to make such a claim?

Well, first, I have always been a writer and an editor. Believe it or not, I used to hunch in front of a manual typewriter, bashing out copy, when my landlady hammered on the door of my flat screeching for her rent. I wouldn't say I was ever in danger of winning a Pulitzer Prize, but you are listening to the first reviewer of the first Led Zeppelin album; the founder of a popular cookery column called "Poverty Cooking"; and the first biographer of both Bruce Lee and Muhammad Ali—which books, by the way, sold five million copies around the world long before most of you were born.

Then again, more recently, I amused myself by helping to write many of the front-cover lines on various editions of *Maxim*. "How to Score at a Funeral," "Xena Like You've Never Seen Her," and "Office Sex, Your Desk or Mine" are among my proud *Maxim* headline achievements.

I'm also the author of a recent anti-self help book, *How to Get Rich*, a number one best-seller in Britain soon to be published here in the United States by Penguin Portfolio. I highly recommend it to those of you who truly desire to be richer than the chump sitting next to you. I'll be selling copies for those wise enough to purchase one at the completion of this lecture.

Lastly, I'm one of Britain's best-selling poets. Yes, I know, it's a hard thing to believe, but it's true. My poetry has even been performed by the Royal Shakespeare Company. I take writing poetry seriously, and for the last seven years have spent an average of three hours each day studying or writing verse.

Here is a sample of one of my poems, a sonnet that might have been written for almost every person here today. Its subject is the general quality of nonacademic writing standards in English in recent years, at least to my eyes, and the pernicious effects of the decline in those standards, especially growing illiteracy and the growth of semiliteracy encouraged by e-mailing, texting, and electronic communication generally. It is dedicated to the immortal memory of a lad from my hometown, Stratford-upon-Avon, one William Shakespeare. I have had the honor of this poem being read by Anton Lessor, one of the finest Shakespearian actors alive today, at a performance by the Royal Shakespeare Company at the Globe Theatre. The central conceit of the poem is that words are like wine. I am not as good a reader as Mr. Lessor, but here's my best shot:

WILL IS DEAD

Abandoned vineyards leave but little trace;
Untrodden cellars leach away their joys;

Our dialect—the glory of our race—
Breeds noble rot that sickens and destroys,
A feeble sediment to salt the bread
Of half a hundred tongues. Let it be so.
To live there must be will, yet Will is dead.
Our vintages decline; our stock is low.

No scholar I. Perhaps I but mistake
The rap of master vintners at the door—
A pretty thought! But, oh, this stuff we make
Is residue of wine too long in store,
     And in my heart I fear the muse has fled.
     Our words are watered wine;
           and Will is dead.

So much for my writing credentials.

As far as publishing is concerned, I started my company thirty-five years ago in London with a hundred bucks in the bank. Over the years, my publishing activities have earned me hundreds of millions of dollars— much of which, I am proud to say, I spent as fast as we earned it.

All together, I believe I have launched, acquired, bought, sold, and folded more than 120 magazines, together with innumerable one-shots. Today, I remain the sole owner of Dennis Publishing, which publishes 50-odd magazines and Web sites. We have been active in the United States since 1975, when I published a licensed one-shot for the movie *Jaws*. Dennis titles you may have heard of include *Star Hits*, *MacUser*, *Computer Shopper*, *Evo*, *Maxim*, *Blender*, and *The First Post*. Dennis's biggest brand today is a magazine called *The Week*, of which more later.

Those then are my publishing credentials.

Let us return to the issue of the reader as king. Undoubtedly it has been my company's adherence to this philosophy which has sustained us through thick and thin. Relentless focus on what readers want (even if they don't know they want it yet) has set me apart from most other publishers of magazines, whose real concern, it seems to me, is what their advertisers want. This focus on what the reader wants as opposed to what advertisers want has somehow turned me into an "iconoclast" and a "contrarian." Or a "maverick." You will find those words associated with my name in hundreds of interviews and articles on the Web and elsewhere. In fact, creating products whose primary goal is to satisfy my readers' desire for entertainment and information led *The Wall Street Journal* to ask in a large 2001 headline, "Is Felix Dennis Mad?"

Maybe. But I am also a damn sight richer than a hell of a lot of saner rivals. These rivals have watched, bewildered, while a magazine like *Maxim* wiped the floor with every other men's lifestyle magazine in America.

Maxim, for example, still sells more than most of its rivals' circulations combined. And that isn't the only time we've done it. *Blender* is knocking on the circulation door of dear old *Rolling Stone*. *MacUser* was such a threat to Ziff-Davis's dominance of the PC marketplace 20-odd years ago that Bill Ziff, one of the finest magazine publishers who ever lived, paid me the then incredible sum of $23 million to acquire it. And today . . . ah, we'll return the future presently.

So, no; I'm *not* mad. What's madness is thinking that you can publish on and on and on without putting out something that readers want to read. What's madness is this: focusing on what advertisers want, not on what readers want. Using cheap or zero-remit subscriptions to round up disinterested readers on whom to foist those products. Focusing on what will impress fellow writers and editors and rounding up advertisers to support it. Droning on about declining circulations.

Instead, U.S. editors wink at the ad-driven content they have to run for the business guys. And the business guys wink at the indulgent content the editors run to win awards. Meanwhile, the reader is nodding off or surfing the Web.

This is why so many magazines have lost their way. They are owned by huge conglomerates or venture capitalists, few of whom have any interest in building long-term, sustainable magazine or Web brands. They are locked in an endless cycle of comparing this month's figures with last month's figures and this year's figures with last year's figures. They want financial results. Correction. They *need* financial results—and they need them now.

And, of course, the Internet is the revenge of the reader. The "threat" of the Internet is not merely the advance of one medium (digital) against another (print). The Internet is disruptive not just as a new means of delivering content but because we can now track what people actually read. This is a catastrophe for those editors and writers who wish, above everything, to assure the plaudits of their peers by winning awards.

It is also a catastrophe for those who practice arcane arts in magazine circulation departments. Just as many hedge funds are currently being exposed as exotic swindles and leveraged hogwash (their crash predicted eighteen months ago in my book, *How to Get Rich*), so the Web exposes and makes redundant zero-remit subscription practitioners in the back rooms of magazine companies. Because most content on the Web is free, these so-called circulation "experts" are now busy concocting a whole bunch of new and dubious techniques in order to pretend to advertisers that the tedious content on their sites really *is* of interest to viewers. But it's hard on them, brothers and sisters. It's hard. Much harder than it used to be, when the vast majority of subscriptions for certain magazines in the United States of America were "sold" for virtually nothing by the delivery of an envelope with a sly slogan on the front: "You have won a million dollars!" Oh, *sure* you have.

I said I'd return to speak about *The Week*.

The Week, in essence, is a précis of last week's news from hundreds of disparate news sources around the world. Just as aeronautical engineers tell us bumblebees are not supposed to be able to fly, even though they've been doing so for millions of years, so *The Week* goes from strength to strength on both sides of the Atlantic. Like the Web, it just grows and grows while its rivals, *Time* and *Newsweek*, have lost a million subscribers between them.

We'll be launching a third edition of *The Week* for Asia and Oceania, later this fall. As both an ink-on-paper and a Web product.

Readers of *The Week* don't just *like* the magazine. They literally proselytize. They buy subscriptions for their friends and family. They write us in their thousands telling us "not to change a single thing in the magazine, you hear?" I hear them. I have always heard them. They are my bread, my butter, my caviar, and my Gulfstream jet. (Er, actually, I always rent the private jets. My rule is, if it flies, floats, or fornicates, rent it. It's cheaper in the long run.)

So why has *The Week* reached half a million copies in the United States from a standing start, while other news and opinion magazines have stumbled in the same short period? Why did Samir Husni, the Internet's Mr. Magazine and professor of journalism at the University of Mississippi (boooo!) choose *The Week* as the most notable U.S. launch of the year in 2002? Why did Barry Diller say, "*The Week* is a perfect magazine—I wouldn't change a thing"? Why, for that matter, do the "100 Most Powerful People in the UK Media" vote *The Week* as their number one magazine over and over? Why is *The Week* the favorite magazine of hundreds of journalists and editors from Chicago to New Delhi, from Dublin to Washington, D.C.? Why did David Carr in *The New York Times*, writing about his own household, say: "Reading matter piles up . . . but *The Week* is read"?

Simple. *The Week* is reader-driven. Utterly reader-driven. No ifs. No buts. No little "compromises." No slippery slope from which there is no return. The reader is king at *The Week*. And *The Week* is essential to its readers.

Now, I like to thank my advertisers. I appreciate their custom, just as they appreciate the quality of reader *The Week* brings to them. My advertisers are welcome to attend the party. *But they are not the guests of honor.* They are welcome to a glass of champagne and piece of the cake, but I am married to my readers and not to my advertisers.

At Dennis, we look for journalists and editors who *put the reader first every time.*

I'm not speaking here about not sucking up to advertisers and editorial independence. Those are important issues, sure. But vastly more important is the ability of an editorial person to *put themselves in the shoes of the reader* and *provide what the reader wants, whether or not the reader knew what they wanted before they opened the magazine.*

This ability is the magic bullet to professional success.

We have one editor at Dennis Publishing who barely wanders into the office but once a week, or even once a month. He works "at home," i.e., mostly down the pub. His readers adore him, but he is a pain in the butt to our senior managers. He's difficult. He's cantankerous. He yells at management. He yells at anyone. He is a prima donna. He reminds me of me.

So what? We're big grown-up boys and girls at Dennis, and we love talent more than we love a stable and efficient environment. We will literally put up with anything (except playing with matches and gasoline) in order to acquire and nurture editorial talent *that knows what the reader wants and gives it to them, issue after issue.*

And just how important can this really be?

Well, as I told you, Dennis Publishing started 36 years ago with 50 quid in the bank. We didn't even have the first month's rent, let alone any money for salaries. But thanks to constantly putting our readers first and checking our own egos at reception every morning, Dennis Publishing has provided me personally with hundreds of millions of dollars, which I have obligingly squandered and hosed away on wine, women, sex, drugs, rock 'n' roll, real estate, art and . . . even . . . the odd bonus or two to the people who made it all happen. Not just to the suits, but to writers and journalists and editors too. Boys and girls just like you.

Journalists and editors are the lifeblood of our industry. Every media owner will say that publicly. But how many of them put their money where their mouth is behind the boardroom door? Look around you. Look at the great names in newspapers and magazines in America today. What do you see? You see layoffs. You see cuts—nearly always in the newsroom or the writers' and editors' bullpen. It's an easy way for the suits and business people to make their numbers. Only on the Internet is there meaningful growth in the number of writers and journalists being employed. Maybe that's one of the reasons the Web is relentlessly gaining on ink-on-paper media.

Well, the hell with that. I enjoy making money as much as the next guy, but what appears to be happening in the magazine and newspaper industry in Europe and America makes little sense to me. While we are busy building our Web assets relentlessly at Dennis Publishing, I remain consistent to the mantra that has served me so well for so many decades. The reader is king. Never forget it. Never compromise. Worship no other idol. If you look after the reader, your readers will look after you.

And maybe, just maybe, that is why, in 2007, Dennis Publishing made more money in the UK than we have made since before most of you were born.

So, here is heresy number three. The world is changing. Do not always listen to old hands who've been in the game for years, including yours truly. Do not blindly heed their well- meaning advice. Read their work and watch their work habits. Always do your homework. Do not be a smart-aleck or treat your readers as a commodity. *Put yourself in your reader's shoes. Give them what they want and what they need.*

Always, always, always pause to consider: What is it my reader needs? What is it my reader wants? What will get readers buying this magazine or visiting this site over and over again?

Then—and only then, when you're convinced you have the answer—should you fight your corner like a demon. In next to no time, if you are working for the right company, you'll find yourself promoted and your name racing up the masthead. Before you know where you are, at our company anyway, you'll probably find yourself in the terrifying position of having achieved godlike editor-in-chief status.

It isn't rocket science or something you're born with. *It comes from empathy with your readers.* And if the company you work for will not recognize that and prefers a quiet corporate life without annoying interruptions from uppity editorial juniors, my advice is simple: leave 'em. You won't learn anything worthwhile there, no matter what they pay you.

And now two commercial messages. First, I hear that the editor-at-large of *Newsweek* was here recently bleating on about how upset he was that not one of the 100-odd students in attendance read his magazine. Lordy, lordy! Horror of horrors! Here's my plea: until you are earning a decent salary, can I please ask you not to subscribe to *The Week*. I do not want you lot buggering up my reader demographic on *The Week*. Not unless your rich uncle has left you a sizable fortune already, that is. However, should you wish to receive a free year's trial subscription of *The Week*, just give me your home address after this lecture and I'll take care of it.

Message number two: Learn your craft first. Learn how to become a great reader-driven writer and a great reader-driven editor. Read *How to Get Rich* to understand why it is a dumb idea to rush off and launch your own Web site or magazine *before* you hve mastered your craft.

After all, I wrote *How to Get Rich* for you lot—much of it is about our industry. I do not want to see you making all the dumb errors I made. Either through luck or through genius, you've chosen a bulletproof and virtually futureproof profession. No need to screw it up by trying to run before you can walk.

And if you believe *that*, then you haven't been listening to a word I've been saying. What *How to Get Rich* actually preaches is this: Go for it. Go for it *now*. *Don't* wait. *Don't* prevaricate. Give it all you've got. Listen to older and wiser heads—and then ignore the old farts.

You are the future of American journalism. Our magazines and sites are in your hands—or will be shortly. Jut remember to keep the seat of your pants applied to the seat of the chair. And hang your ego and your political and religious beliefs up with your coat when you arrive at work each day.

I hope to see every one of your names in print. At the top of the masthead!

Acknowledgments

The editors would like to acknowledge the contributions of those magazine editors published in these pages and the many others who have delivered Delacorte lectures over the past dozen years and more. We would also like to thank Barbara Fasciani of the Columbia Journalism School, who helped facilitate the events at Columbia and the transcription of the talks, and Mary Schilling of *The Nation*, who, as always, made the trains run on time. Zohar Kadmon Sella, a graduate student at Columbia, provided invaluable editorial assistance to the project, and over the years, Brian Gallagher, Anya Schiffrin, José Leyva, and Hilke Schellmann helpfully oversaw speaker arrivals and departures.

Philip Leventhal at Columbia University Press has been a patient and helpful collaborator during the development of this book, and Leslie Kriesel helped immensely with the final steps along the way. Finally, we wish to thank those many Columbia Journalism School students whose pertinent—and even impertinent—questions at the lectures helped draw out fascinating insights from our speakers, and who have made the entire process a reward for those of us involved in putting these lectures on.